URBANIZATION IN AUSTRALIA

THE NINETEENTH CENTURY

EDITED BY

C. B. SCHEDVIN &
J. W. McCARTY

SYDNEY UNIVERSITY PRESS

SYDNEY UNIVERSITY PRESS
Press Building, University of Sydney

UNITED KINGDOM, EUROPE, MIDDLE EAST, AFRICA, CARIBBEAN
Prentice/Hall International, International Book Distributors Ltd
Hemel Hempstead, England

NORTH AND SOUTH AMERICA
International Scholarly Book Services, Inc., Portland, Oregon

First published 1970 in *Australian Economic History Review*
Reprinted in book form 1974 by Sydney University Press

National Library of Australia registry card number and
ISBN 0 424 06940 7

This book is supported by money from
The Eleanor Sophia Wood Bequest

Printed in Australia by Southwood Press Pty Limited Sydney

2.25

CONTENTS

PREFACE

The interest of historians in particular aspects of the past often reflects the current concerns of the society in which they live and write. In Australia, the experience of the 1930s depression led Brian Fitzpatrick and others to write Australian history in terms of class struggle. In the late 1960s and 1970s a growing realization by Australians of the importance of cities, of the costs and inconvenience of living in them, has led some of our ablest historians to study the history of their cities, and to think of Australian history in terms of relationships between cities and their rural hinterlands. Economic historians have become interested in Australian urban history mainly because of the work of N. G. Butlin,[1] who documented the simple, indeed obvious point that urban areas, especially capital cities, have always accounted for a large share of Australian population, investment and production. It is evident, too, that they have played an important, perhaps dominant, rôle in our social and political history. At the very least, a sense of proportion requires that they can no longer be ignored in any general view of Australian history.

The first two essays in this book, first published as a special issue of *Australian Economic History Review* (September 1970), address themselves to aspects of N. G. Butlin's work. J. W. McCarty describes population growth in the Australian capital cities in the nineteenth century in relation to the population of their colonies, and also argues that the Australian cities were representatives of a general type of 'commercial city' that appeared in new regions of settlement. R. V. Jackson questions Butlin's view that in late nineteenth-century Australia half or more of the Australian people owned rather than rented their houses. Jackson analyses rate books, an important source for urban historians, to show that only 30 per cent of houses in parts

[1] *Investment in Australian Economic Development 1861-1900*, Cambridge 1964.

of Sydney were owner-occupied in 1891.[2]

The building of the residential suburbs so typical of Australian cities required the services of developers, familiar to city-dwellers today, who subdivided large old estates for urban expansion. The history of 'eight acres' in the Sydney suburb of Paddington in the 1880s is a detailed illustration of the developer at work. Paddington was an inner suburb within walking distance of the city centre; expansion to outer suburbs of large cities depended, as Davison shows in his essay on 'Public Utilities and the Expansion of Melbourne in the 1880s', on a corresponding extension of transport and other public utilities.[3]

The remaining three essays direct attention to urban areas other than capital cities. Daly's study of Newcastle illustrates the important contribution that historical geography can make to the study of urban history.[4] Bate discusses some recent writing on country towns, and stresses the importance of setting the city, or country town, in its proper regional context. Much less work has been done in Australian than British or American urban history, but Glynn warns Australian historians against the uncritical borrowing of overseas methodology.

Some important books on Australian urban history have been published recently. Sean Glynn, *Urbanisation in Australian History* (Melbourne 1970) is an interesting historical survey, and H. Stretton, *Ideas for Australian Cities* (Adelaide 1970) is a fascinating discussion of Australian capital cities today which looks – too briefly for historians – at the origins of our present urban chaos. J. Grant and G. Serle, *The Melbourne Scene 1803-1956* (Melbourne 1957) and A. Birch and D. S. Macmillan, *The Sydney Scene 1788-1960* (Melbourne 1962), contain much interesting information in the form of contemporary documents. Students of Melbourne's history can also read three excellent histories of suburbs: W. Bate, *A History of Brighton* (Melbourne 1962); G. N. Blainey, *A History of Camberwell* (Melbourne 1964); B. Barrett, *The Inner Suburbs* (Melbourne 1971).

[2] A. E. Dingle and D. T. Merrett have shown that in Melbourne about 40 per cent of people owned their own homes in 1891 and 1911; but, as in Sydney, tenancy was much higher in poor than well-off suburbs. 'Home Owners and Tenants in Melbourne, 1891-1911', *Australian Economic History Review,* Vol. XII, No. 1 (March 1972).

[3] A revised version of this essay forms a chapter in Davison's forthcoming book *The Rise and Fall of Marvellous Melbourne.*

[4] For a criticism of this article, and a reply by Daly, see *Australian Economic History Review,* Vol. XI, No. 2 (September 1971).

Preface

Three important recent books illustrate quite different ways of writing the history of a city. P. Bolger's *Hobart Town* (Canberra 1973) captures the changing social and intellectual climate of the middle classes of nineteenth-century Hobart, a small and inward-looking urban community. J. B. Hirst in *Adelaide and the Country 1870-1917* (Melbourne 1973) has chosen not to write the story of Adelaide itself but the history of its changing economic, social and political relationships with its countryside, and has shown the value of writing South Australian, and perhaps Australian history, from this perspective. R. Lawson's *Brisbane in the 1890s* (St Lucia 1973) is a detailed study notable for its imaginative use of sociological concepts. On country towns, mention should be made of S. Priestley, *Echuca* (Brisbane 1965) and *Warracknabeal* (Brisbane 1967), and K. Swan, *A History of Wagga Wagga* (Wagga Wagga 1970), as well as chapters in the regional histories by Buxton, Waterson and others discussed by Bate in this book.

May 1974 C.B.S.

J.W.McC.

CONTRIBUTORS

Weston Bate	Senior Lecturer in History, University of Melbourne
M. T. Daly	Senior Lecturer in Earth Sciences, Macquarie University
Graeme Davison	Lecturer in History, University of Melbourne
Sean Glynn	Lecturer in Economic and Social History, University of Kent at Canterbury
R. V. Jackson	Lecturer in Economic History, Australian National University
M. J. Kelly	Lecturer in History, Macquarie University
J. W. McCarty	Professor of Economic History, Monash University
C. B. Schedvin	Reader in Economic History, Monash University

J. W. McCarty

AUSTRALIAN CAPITAL CITIES IN THE NINETEENTH CENTURY

I

A principal virtue of the literary approach to history is that the historian can permit himself the luxury of omitting from his story difficult if relevant topics. Edward Shann and Brian Fitzpatrick wrote their economic histories of Australia without making more than passing mention of the capital cities, and their example has been followed by later historians such as Professor Russel Ward whose book *Australia* (1965) indexes the 'Melbourne Cup' but not 'Melbourne'. Sociologists tell us that the inhabitants of large cities become anonymous as individuals, but this cannot be held to be true of them as a group, for the six capital cities contained one-quarter of the Australian population in 1871 and one-third in 1901. They were the points of entry and of permanent residence for most immigrants; they were the centres of government and of colonial trade, finance and transport. Yet as the nineteenth century enters its final decade—one of depression in which, however, the capital cities increased slightly their percentage share of total population and further consolidated their control over the rural hinterlands—we find most Australian historians gazing fixedly at the countryside. The economic historians describe the pastoral collapse 'back of Bourke', the social historians the tribulations of the pastoral workers and miners, and the literary historians the writings of Henry Lawson and his friends most of whom could be removed only forcibly from the Sydney bars they loved so well to the great outback about which they wrote so well.

One reason for the neglect of Australian urban history is that its subject matter cannot be fitted easily into any of the compartments of traditional historiography. Political historians, for example, usually write in a colonial or national context, and social historians in a class context; economic historians delimit their subject matter in terms of firms or industries or a chronological period of a colony or nation. The city does not fit into these classifications and the urban-rural division often cuts across them, so that urban history, lacking any generally accepted method of analysis of its own, has been unable to claim the attention of the historian. It is significant that much of the best overseas work on urban history, where the subject is more advanced than in Australia, has been pre-empted—by default of the historians—by sociologists, historical geographers, economists and town planners. Such work although valuable lacks the cohesion and sense of change through time that can be supplied only by an historical approach, provided of course that the urban historian has access to appropriate methods of analysis.

Lack of suitable techniques cannot however be considered to be a sufficient explanation for the neglect of Australian urban history, for this has never in the past deterred our historians from investigating subjects that interested them. A second reason may be that urban history lacks an ideological interest that has been so important in Australian historiography. The evolution of the Australian political structure and national identity, the rise of the labour movement, the development of the rural export industries, the role of the state in economic life and similar themes have dominated historians' interests but have not required them to examine the history of the capital cities. If the study of grand themes has bypassed the cities, so too has the study of local history, which has made a humbler but equally important contribution to Australian historical research.

It is to local historians that we owe what work there is on Australian cities and towns. A complete list of anecdotal histories of towns and suburbs would run into several hundreds; to these have been added in recent years a small number of books that meet the highest standards of historical scholarship. Mr Bate's *History of Brighton* and Professor Blainey's *History of Camberwell* describe the life of two rural villages that became, towards the end of the nineteenth century, residential suburbs of Melbourne. Both historians devote most of their attention to the earlier period, when the economic and social life of the villages was essentially self-contained, thus providing a central historical theme that each historian has used to good effect. The theme disappeared, however, as Brighton and Camberwell changed from villages to commuter suburbs, for each suburb then had no identity and no history except in its relationship to the city of which it was a part. Mr Bate and Professor Blainey were obliged to stop their histories at that point for they now lacked a coherent subject. Their historical method, appropriate to the study of small, essentially self-contained communities, is inappropriate to the study of a city, for which the appropriate method seems to be to analyse the growth of the city as a whole in terms of the changing relationships of its component parts, especially of the city core and its suburbs.

The local historian quite properly emphasizes the unique features of his chosen small community rather than the characteristics that it shares with similar groups, but this practice is inappropriate when the unit of study is the city rather than the village, or the nation rather than the region. Australian historians, by failing to use properly the comparative method of history, have often got themselves unnecessarily into difficulties by assuming that the history of their own country is unique. The Australian colonies in the nineteenth century belonged to a group of rapidly growing new countries, including the United States and Canada, Argentina and New Zealand, that Ragnar Nurkse called 'regions of recent settlement'. Although the similarity of their political histories may not be immediately evident, that of their economic histories is, for they had similar natural resources and played similar roles in the world economy as exporters of primary products.[1] The capital cities were even more alike than their regions. Their economic and social structures tended to vary as their rural hinterlands varied, but as commercial cities linking the hinterlands to world markets, each was fully exposed to the levelling effects of the expanding world capitalist economy.

II

The main characteristics of the Australian capital cities can be most readily identified by placing them in a general world typology of cities in the nineteenth century. If one eliminates from consideration Asian and other cities that were only marginally affected by the expansion of European capitalism, three groups of cities remain. Most European cities which originated in Roman or medieval times were still affected, in the nineteenth century, by their prior development. The early geographical and institutional history of London, for example, continued to influence the pattern of its growth in later centuries, and its history may well be written around the theme of the efforts to transform or demolish the legacy of the past: obsolete buildings, roads and bridges; guilds and other forms of government that resisted political change; forms of industrial organization that impeded innovation. Traditional theories of urban growth have attempted to explain how such cities evolved, in response to the rise of capitalist modes of production, to their modern forms. Max Weber, for example, investigated the social and power structures of such cities in transition; Thunen developed the first general theory of urban economic growth to explain the transition of a town and its agricultural hinterland from subsistence to capitalistic production; and medieval historians have investigated

1 Nurkse's essays on this subject are collected in *Equilibrium and Growth in the World Economy*, Harvard 1961. On comparative political history see L. Hartz (ed.), *The Founding of New Societies*, New York 1964.

the struggles of the cities to win independence from feudal lords. The central theme of these theories of urban growth is the gradual emergence of cities from their inferior status in pre-capitalistic agrarian societies. With the growth of trade and industry, the spread of a money economy, and the gradual conversion of the countryside from subsistence to cash farming, the positions of country and city were reversed. The city came to dominate its rural hinterland, and itself underwent internal change.

Traditional cities evolved in ways that require methods of historical analysis that are not appropriate to Australian cities, which are 'pure' products of the nineteenth-century expansion of capitalism. Nor is the traditional methodology appropriate to a second important type of city: the manufacturing city created by the industrial revolution. As cotton manufacture largely determined the rate of growth and economic and social structure of Manchester in the nineteenth century, so the rise of iron and steel production dominated the urban history of Pittsburgh. In such cases, industrialization induced urbanization and urban history is best written around the history of the dominant industry. In contrast, a striking characteristic of the 'commercial cities' is that industrialization followed urbanization, and the rise of manufactures cannot therefore be used to explain urban growth. The primary economic function of these cities was to act as bases for the opening up of new lands. Manufacturing was often an important industry in these cities, but was induced by population growth, and by the linked demands of service and export industries, giving rise to railway workshops, foundries, ship repair yards, agricultural implement factories, packing and freezing works, and so on.[2] The growth of the commercial cities was determined predominantly by world economic forces, and by the broadly similar requirements of the staple export economies that formed their hinterlands. For these reasons one would expect them as a group to exhibit stronger likenesses and regularities in their structure and growth than either the pre-capitalistic cities, each differing according to its prior history, or the industrial cities, each differing according to the nature of its dominant manufacturing industry.

The first noticeable characteristic of the commercial cities compared to the other types is that they were established at a moment of time, and at once assumed an important and often dominant role in the new region. When American settlers crossed the Appalachian mountains in the late eighteenth century, 'the establishment of towns preceded the

[2] Commercial cities such as Chicago and some other American cities sometimes evolved into predominantly industrial cities if manufacturing was able to develop from a dependent to an autonomous role in the city economy, but this did not occur in Australia in the nineteenth century.

breaking of the soil. . . . The towns were the spearheads of the frontier.' Professor Richard Morse, discussing the origins of Latin American towns, writes that 'to anyone steeped in the history of European cities, their organic growth and their slow sedimentation of function, the act of founding a town in the New World wilderness and in a moment of time will seem almost gratuitous'.[3] In Australia in the nineteenth century as in Latin America in the sixteenth, the towns and government were planted first and the hinterlands developed later, and—also as in the Americas—the cities were usually established with only small and often inaccurate knowledge of the resources and possibilities of economic development of the hinterlands. This was the case with the establishment of Sydney, Hobart and Launceston, and Brisbane, which were, admittedly, established as convict rather than commercial cities. Perth, Melbourne, and Adelaide may, however, be considered examples of 'pure' commercial cities that were established with only limited prior investigation of their locational possibilities. Initial errors in the choice of location, or unforeseen changes in the economic pattern, such as the discovery of minerals or introduction of new rural industries, may thus work against the planted city. This was particularly evident in Latin America owing to the instability of the sort of commercial capitalism that developed there, to the warping effects of Spanish mercantilist policy, and to the persistence of large semi-subsistence agricultural and pastoral regions in the more remote parts of the continent, all of which restrained or distorted the growth of the coastal 'commercial cities'. The absence of such factors in Australia may help to explain the historical stability and continued dominance of the Australian capitals all of which—with the possible exception of Hobart—consolidated their initial dominance over their hinterlands, despite considerable economic changes during the nineteenth century.

Some reasons for this dominance are mentioned later in this essay; here we are concerned to question the view that the Australian cities were abnormally large. Contemporaries such as G. R. Parkin and T. A. Coghlan were quite definite:

> Population flocks into the towns of Australia in a proportion not known anywhere else. Melbourne contains nearly one-half of the people of Victoria, Sydney more than a third of the population of New South Wales. In all the colonies the capital cities grow in like proportion at the expense of the smaller towns and country districts. That the increase of urban population . . . should find its greatest

[3] Richard C. Wade, *The Urban Frontier: The Rise of Western Cities, 1790-1830*, Harvard 1959, p. 1; and Richard M. Morse, 'Some Characteristics of Latin American Urban History', *American Historical Review*, Vol. LXVII, No. 2 (January 1962), p. 321.

> excess in this new country is a peculiar fact . . .
>
> The progress of the chief cities of Australia . . . has no parallel among the cities of the old world. Even in America the rise of the great cities has been accompanied by a corresponding increase in the rural population . . . The abnormal aggregation of the [Australian] population into their capital cities is a most unfortunate element in the progress of the colonies.[4]

More recently, Professor N. G. Butlin has written:

> As early as 1891, this new and underdeveloped area had succeeded in carrying urbanization to a degree which was rare in the rest of the world. Almost two-thirds of the population of 1891 lived in towns and cities, a proportion which was not matched by other 'new' countries, particularly the United States, until 1920, and Canada until 1950.[5]

Professor Butlin's view cannot be considered conclusive unless the official statistics are recalculated to ensure comparability. In 1891, for example, the minimum official size for a New South Wales town was 500, and for a United States town 8,000; many New South Wales municipalities were large areas that included more rural than urban inhabitants yet all were counted as urban; and the point of particular relevance is that the United States census figures consistently understated the size of cities owing to their failure to identify all suburban areas. In 1891 San Francisco's 'official' population of 299,000 was 18 per cent below Davis and Langlois' careful recent estimate of 364,000 which includes areas that were suburban, but not considered so under the census definition.[6] San Francisco seems to be the American city most directly comparable with Melbourne and Sydney. Its population increased rapidly in the 1850s owing to gold rushes, and in 1891 was 364,000, compared to 473,000 in Melbourne and 400,000 in Sydney; it had similar economic functions as an entrepôt for its hinterland. Another commercial city, Buenos Aires, may be added to the comparison, which casts some doubt on (but does not contravert conclusively) the present view.

[4] G. R. Parkin, 'Australian Cities', *The Colonial Century*, March 1891, p. 690; T. A. Coghlan, *The Seven Colonies of Australasia, 1895-96*, p. 47. See also W. P. Reeves, *State Experiments in Australia and New Zealand*, Vol. I, London 1902, p. 35: 'For a young country, Australia has a curiously large city population.'

[5] N. G. Butlin, *Investment in Australian Economic Development 1861-1900*, Cambridge 1964, p. 181.

[6] K. Davis and E. Langlois, *Future Demographic Growth of the San Francisco Bay Area*, Berkeley 1963, p. 7. The authors include suburbs that are officially part of neighbouring counties. The standard work by A. F. Weber, *The Growth of Cities in the Nineteenth Century*, Columbia 1899, must be used with caution for this reason.

Table 1

Three Commercial Cities, 1871 to 1911

Year	Sydney		San Francisco		Buenos Aires		
	I	II	I	II	I	II(a)	II(b)
1871	138	27	163	29	180	36	17
1891	400	35	364	30	—	—	—
1911	648	47	670	28	3,600	42	24

I Population in thousands.

II Population as a percentage of their regions. The regions for Sydney and San Francisco are New South Wales and California. For Buenos Aires, the region for II(a) is the province of Buenos Aires; that for II(b) is the larger area of the five coastal provinces of Buenos Aires, Santa Fe, Cordoba, Entre Dios, and Corrientes. The low percentage of San Francisco in 1911 was due to the rapid growth of Los Angeles' population to 319,000 in that year.

Sources: *Sydney*: Appendix; San Francisco: Davis and Langlois, op. cit.; Buenos Aires: James R. Scobie, *Argentina: A City and a Nation*, New York 1964.

Economic dominance may alternatively be assessed by using the geographers' concept of primacy, which measures the population of the largest city as a ratio of the next largest (or four next largest) in a region, and finds a lack of cities of intermediate size. In Australia in 1900, Brisbane had 7 times the population of Rockhampton, its nearest rival, and Sydney 9 times the population of Newcastle; Perth and Melbourne had ratios of 10 and 11, and Adelaide a ratio of 23 to 1. Hobart had only one-third more population than Launceston. In other countries, San Francisco had 4½ times the population of Los Angeles and Buenos Aires had (in 1911) 7 times the population of Rosario. 'Commercial' cities are primate, but so too are Asian cities and the latter have captured the attention of geographers. Comparison of city groups throughout the world suggests that they fall into either a primate or into a rank distribution with a fairly uniform progression from small to large cities. The conclusion derived from this evidence is that rank distributions characterize economically developed countries, whereas primate distributions characterize over-urbanization, usually in underdeveloped countries. Primate cities in Asian countries are said to have stunting effects upon the development of smaller urban places and tend to be parasitic in relation to the remainder of the regional economy. This criticism reminds one of Parkin and Coghlan and seems to lend support to them. It is, however, based on a misreading of the evidence. Professor Berry has recently re-examined the world evidence and concluded that 'different city size distributions are in no way related to the relative economic development of countries'; he suggests that primate distributions reflect *simplicity* of economic structure resulting from the operation of a few dominant economic forces, while rank distributions reflect more complex economic patterns, such as occur in most industrialized countries. In this sense, the Australian and Asian economies were similar, the former being dominated by rural export industries and the latter by peasant agriculture.[7] A further objection to city distribution theory is that the resulting distribution often depends on the definition of the region. The primate distribution of Australian capital cities disappears to a large extent if the colonies are amalgamated into an Australian region, and San Francisco, a primate city in California, becomes part of a rank distribution in the United States. Australian cities were large, but they were not therefore abnormal.

A third characteristic of commercial cities is to be found in their internal geographical and economic structures. The geography of traditional cities at any point of time in the nineteenth century was a palimpsest of centuries of change with newer patterns of housing, shops and factories and transport systems superimposed on or adapted to previous patterns, so that the cities differed significantly, as did the industrial cities according to the nature of their dominant industries. By contrast it is the similarity of the commercial cities rather than their differences that is the more striking characteristic.

In a long perspective the historical geography of the commercial cities may be divided into three periods, defined by their size in relation to the available means of transport. In the first period, from their varying dates of foundation to the 1870s or 1880s, the cities were 'walking' cities owing to the high cost of land transport. Rich people lived in the city centre in a setting that was not yet spoiled by nearby shops, factories and office buildings, although some, who preferred the life of a 'country' gentleman and could afford daily private transport to the city, built houses in the surrounding countryside. Office and factory workers had to live within walking distance of their work, either in the city centre (or near the port, if, as in Melbourne, Adelaide or Perth, this was some miles removed from the city centre) or in immediately adjoining suburbs that developed as the city grew. These 'inner' suburbs generally differentiated themselves into two types, those which became industrial working class suburbs with a dense mixture of factories, warehouses and workers' cottages, and those which became more purely

[7] B. J. L. Berry, 'City Size Distributions and Economic Development', *Economic Development and Cultural Change*, Vol. IX, No. 4 (July 1961), pp. 573-87, reprinted in J. Friedmann and W. Alonso (eds), *Regional Development and Planning*, MIT Press, 1964. For a review of city distribution theory see R. W. Chorley and P. Haggett (eds), *Socio-Economic Models in Geography*, London 1967, Chapter 9. For the point in the following sentence see A. J. Rose, 'Dissent from Down Under: Metropolitan Primacy as the Normal State', *Pacific Viewpoint*, Vol. IV (1963), pp. 163-8.

residential suburbs for middle class and white collar workers. In Melbourne, Carlton and Fitzroy were examples of the latter type so long as they could withstand encroachment by neighbouring industrial suburbs; Paddington and North Sydney in Sydney, and Kensington and Unley in Adelaide were quite distinct, in this period, from the industrial suburbs which linked with them, geography and town planning permitting, to form a ring around the city centre. The population of the cities thus remained highly concentrated as late as 1880.

Well before the inner zone, consisting of the city core and its adjoining suburbs, was filled in the sense that there was no more land available, the commercial city had begun to expand from the 'walking' to the 'public transport' city by the creation of a new zone of suburbs, which, like the previous zone of inner suburbs, divided themselves into middle and working class suburbs, but with two significant differences. First, the construction of horse or cable tramways and suburban railways and the introduction of cheap fares now enabled workers to travel to work in the inner zone from the new working class residential suburbs such as Leichhardt in Sydney and parts of Brunswick, Footscray and Northcote in Melbourne; these new suburbs contained less industry which continued to locate in the inner zone. Second, residents of the new middle class suburbs opted for larger houses and larger blocks of land, which increased substantially both the cost of the house and associated investment in roads, gas, sewerage and other public utilities. Terraces predominated in Melbourne's inner zone but in the outer zone were greatly outnumbered by detached houses.[8] As the outer zone grew, the inner zone changed. In the city core, the older generation of rich residents emigrated to the new suburbs and their old houses were demolished to make way for retail shops or offices, or were converted into lodging houses. In North American, but not in Australian cities, ghettos in the inner zone housed new migrants with low social as well as economic status. The net effect of these changes was to intensify land use and require heavy new investment in public utilities. The disposal of night soil, not previously an insuperable problem, now required heavy investment in underground sewerage systems, which in

[8] This is evident from an inspection of the detailed survey maps compiled by the Melbourne and Metropolitan Board of Works in the 1890s. Mr D. Saunders uses these maps in his thesis *Terrace Housing in Melbourne* (MArch, University of Melbourne, 1959) to document the high proportion of terraces. Some excellent monographs on the building of new suburbs are available: S. B. Warner, *Streetcar Suburbs: The Process of Growth in Boston 1870-1900*, Harvard 1962, describes the building of a sector of middle class suburbs in southern Boston; H. J. Dyos' study of the suburb of Camberwell in London, *Victorian Suburb*, Leicester 1961, can be profitably compared with G. N. Blainey's *History of Camberwell*, Melbourne 1964.

turn required larger water supplies. Investment in roads, street lighting and public transport increased in the inner as well as outer zones. The construction of houses and public utilities increased the demand for building materials, engineering goods and other manufactures, and so had the effect of creating an autonomous increase in urban investment. Initially, however, the rise of the public transport city depended on two factors: the growing total size of the city, which was due to the general economic growth of the region and especially the export industries; and the high level of income, supported by high consumer tastes, that was generated in the city.[9]

It is not surprising that the phases of expansion just sketched conform reasonably well to E. W. Burgess' concentric-zone theory of the spatial structure of cities, for Burgess based his theory on the growth of Chicago which was in 1924 still predominantly a 'commercial city'.[10] The two essential points of his theory were that the city expanded in concentric zones, and that in the public transport phase the middle class vacated the city centre and jumped over the inner suburbs to a new outer zone of residential suburbs. Burgess' theory generated a large amount of research and, in due course, some criticisms which are relevant to the Australian cities. One is that spatial growth occurs not in concentric zones, but in sectors radiating out from the city core. This seems to follow from the fact that 'commercial cities' are initially located on seafronts or rivers that preclude perfectly concentric expansion, and from the fact that internal public transport routes radiate out from the city core, so inducing a corresponding radial expansion of buildings. Once different types of suburbs are established they perpetuate themselves by expanding along the sector, so that in Adelaide, for example, working class industrial suburbs lie to the west and north-west of the city core, and middle class in the other sectors. This criticism, of great interest to geographers, does not seem to be fundamental from the point of view of the process of economic growth. A second criticism, made by L. F. Schnore, is that the theory does not apply to Latin American cities.[11] The planned cities of colonial Latin America conformed initially to Burgess' scheme, with the rich living

[9] The 'public transport' period lasted until the advent of the automobile after 1945, which is profoundly affecting locational patterns. It has, for example, permitted construction of houses further than walking distance from public transport, broken the dominance of the city core in retailing and the inner suburbs in manufacturing, and permitted workers to live on the urban fringe where land is cheaper. The automobile city does not however concern us in this essay.

[10] E. W. Burgess, 'The Growth of the City', *American Sociological Society*, Vol. XVIII (1924), pp. 85-97, reprinted in R. E. Park (ed.), *The City*, Chicago 1925, pp. 47-62.

[11] 'On the Spatial Structure of Cities in the Two Americas' in P. M. Hansen and L. F. Schnore (eds), *The Study of Urbanization*, New York 1965, Chapter 10.

in the centre and the poor in peripheral slums isolated from the rich by a belt of parklands. As the cities grew in the nineteenth century, houses of the rich spread on to the parkland belt, or across it to push back the slums, but they did not, as in North America, jump the slums to form a new outer zone. Schnore considers that this deviant behaviour was due to the small size of the middle class and to a cultural preference, inherited from the Spanish, for urban rather than rural living. He considers that after about 1900 the rise of a large middle class caused the growth of a sector of middle class housing that cut through the slums to the periphery and so started to rezone the cities on Burgess' theory. Even today, however, the *barrios* of the periphery are a feature that Buenos Aires and other Latin American cities share with Asian cities.

There were large peripheral slums in Latin America but not in North American or Australian cities; there were inner zone ghettos in North American but not in Australian cities. The latter difference may be explained by the hundreds of thousands of European peasants who migrated to the Americas; both differences may be explained by variations in the level of income per head (and in the distribution of income) between the three countries. The dashing colonial statisticians of the late nineteenth century compiled tables which showed that the Australian colonies clearly led all other countries in wealth and gross earnings per head, and Professor N. G. Butlin has recently suggested that Australian incomes per head in the second half of the nineteenth century were substantially higher than at that time in the United States or Britain.[12] The high incomes were made possible by the abundance of natural resources and the productivity of the rural industries that used them. High profits attracted large amounts of capital and relatively lesser amounts of labour from Britain so as to sustain a fast rate of economic growth and, indirectly, the rapid growth of the capital cities. The structure of the cities, with their expensive outer zones of suburbs and public utilities, rested on this foundation.

The Australian commercial city was a new city in which recent economic forces had largely determined its social structure. It had a high degree of social mobility and defined its social classes principally in terms of actual wealth, however acquired, and however recently acquired. The lack of a traditional *élite*, such as existed in European

[12] T. A. Coghlan, *Statistical Account*, 1891, p. 184; R. M. Johnston, *Tasmanian Official Record*, 1892, p. 323. Professor N. G. Butlin has discussed Coghlan's estimates in an unpublished paper 'Return to Plutology'. Although insistent on pointing out the weakness of his data, Professor Butlin's general conclusion seems to me to be clearly proven: 'Long-run Trends in Australian *Per Capita* Consumption' in K. J. Hancock (ed.), *The National Income and Social Welfare*, Melbourne 1965, Chapter 1.

cities, afforded greater freedom and influence to the middle class in the commercial city. Its social structure differed also from that of the industrial city, in which the factory owners ran the city as well as its leading industry. The capitalists formed a homogeneous group, as did the workers, and in both respects the industrial city differed significantly from the commercial city. The characteristic social structure of the latter was a large and fairly dispersed middle class, merging into a working class that also exhibited a wider range of social attitudes and economic circumstances than was to be found in industrial cities. When historians begin to study the social structure of Australian cities it seems probable that the present methods of Australian social history will prove inadequate. If it is true that Australian urban social structure was closely related to economic structure, it may follow that an economic approach to Australian urban history will prove the most useful at this stage of our knowledge.

An urban approach may also throw some light on wider issues in Australian history. Societies that lack an heroic past to sustain them in facing—or ignoring—the realities of their present existence, usually create one suited to their present emotional needs, and often employ historians to do the job. The traditional cities had a rich heritage of Founding Fathers to draw upon, as the older nations had a richer and more distant history from which to create their living legends. The new societies of the nineteenth century in the regions of recent settlement lacked distant pasts from which to draw their legendary emotional sustenance; their cities in particular lacked both historical distance and historical romance, for they had originated rationally and materialistically as full members of an expanding capitalistic system and could not pretend otherwise. Yet their need of a sustaining legend was the stronger, for the closer that the social and emotional life of the urban people was geared to the workings of a capitalistic economic system, the greater was the emotional vacuum of the people, and the greater the need to create their own dream world to escape the monotonous regularity of their present existence.

Unable to turn to their own past, the city people used that of their rural hinterlands for their legends. A frontier did exist in North America, where men were independent and brave; but the legend of the frontier was created in the cities, by serious writers as well as by the hacks who turned out hundreds of Buffalo Bill and Deadwood Dick adventure stories, and who wrote, consciously or unconsciously, to meet a pressing demand for such literature. In the Argentine, the middle and working classes of Buenos Aires created, towards the end of the nineteenth century, the romantic image of the gaucho, and called forth writers to give expression to the myth. In Australia, Ned Kelly and the nomad tribe of bush workers owe their immortality to the urban middle classes and proletariat who dreamed of a way of life that they could never in reality hope to enjoy.[13]

We turn to examine the economic growth of the Australian cities in space and time; and while agreeing with Alfred Marshall that in economic life 'the influence of time is more fundamental than that of space',[14] we are obliged, at this stage of our knowledge, to devote more attention to the historical geography of the cities than to their economic growth.

III

We must now pay more attention to differences between the Australian capital cities than to the similarities that have so far occupied our attention. A taxonomic approach suggests two sets of relationships that seem to form a logical starting point for analysis. Firstly, the six cities may be compared directly with regard to size and rates of growth. This is done in Table 2, which is considered to be more accurate, for reasons given in the Appendix, than T. A. Coghlan's figures that historians have hitherto used.

Table 2

POPULATION OF THE CAPITAL CITIES, 1851 TO 1911

Year	Melbourne		Sydney		Adelaide	
	I	II	I	II	I	II
1851	29	—	54	—	18	—
1861	125	15.7	96	5.9	35	6.9
1871	191	4.3	138	3.7	51	3.9
1881	268	3.4	225	5.0	92	6.1
1891	473	5.8	400	5.9	117	2.4
1901	478	0.1	496	2.2	141	1.9
1911	593	2.2	648	2.7	169	1.8
	Brisbane		**Perth**		**Hobart**	
	I	II	I	II	I	II
1851	3	—	—	—	—	—
1861	6	7.2	5	—	25	—
1871	15	9.6	—	—	26	0.4
1881	31	7.6	9	2.8	27	0.4
1891	94	11.7	16	5.9	33	2.0
1901	119	2.4	61	14.3	35	0.6
1911	141	1.7	107	5.8	40	1.3

I Population in thousands.
II Annual average percentage increase, by decades.
Source: Appendix.

[13] On North American frontier mythology see in particular H. N. Smith, *Virgin Land: The American West as Symbol and Myth*, Harvard 1950. On the gaucho see S. S. Trifilo, 'The Gaucho: His Changing Image', *Pacific Historical Review*, Vol. XXXIII (1964), pp. 395-403, and James R. Scobie's excellent book, *Argentina: A City and a Nation*, New York 1964. On Australia see Russel Ward, *The Australian Legend*, Melbourne 1958.

[14] A. Marshall, *Principles of Economics*, London 1920, p. 496.

The most obvious, if elementary, conclusion to be derived from the table is that the six cities arrange themselves in three pairs. Melbourne and Sydney were clearly the largest cities and were fairly equal in size throughout the period. Adelaide and Brisbane were 'middling' size, although Brisbane was significantly smaller until the 1880s owing to her later start. Perth was very small until 1901; Hobart remained small throughout the period and had a uniquely low rate of growth. There are two arguments that might explain this grouping. The first is that the size and rate of growth of the capital city depends on the wealth and rate of growth of its rural hinterland (or region), and on its ability to dominate the trade, transport, finance, manufacturing, government and other urban activities of the region against the competition of rival cities outside the region, and of other urban centres within the region. Melbourne and Sydney, for example, had large, productive hinterlands in which there were no important urban rivals, but each city competed against the other in urban industries such as manufacturing and shipping, and for control of the Riverina trade; Brisbane had a large but sparser hinterland which it had to share with northern coastal ports; Hobart had a small and stagnant hinterland which it had to share with Launceston; and so on.

The second argument, mentioned earlier in this essay, is that the transition from the walking to the public transport city as a result of population reaching a certain size, which occurred in Melbourne and Sydney in the 1880s and 1890s, necessitates a large *per capita* increase in investment in housing and associated public utilities and linked manufacturing industries. This initiates a process of autonomous growth that further increases the size of the city at the expense of its hinterland. A variation of this argument is that one would expect the cities to grow more rapidly during periods of high investment owing to the labour-saving bias of rural investment and labour-intensive bias of urban investment that has been analysed by Professor N. G. Butlin.

How much will these arguments explain? They require on the one hand an analysis of the growth of the capital cities in a context of the Australian economy, and on the other an analysis of intra-regional relationships between the capital, the countryside and country towns. This second set of relationships involves nothing short of a complete analysis of the regional economies of the period. Table 3, which shows the capital city populations as a percentage of the colonial populations, can be made to support only a few conjectures towards such an analysis.

Melbourne's large population on the eve of the gold rushes illustrates, in somewhat exaggerated form, the importance of the commercial city

Table 3

CAPITAL CITY POPULATION AS A PERCENTAGE OF COLONIAL POPULATION

	Melbourne	Sydney	Adelaide	Brisbane	Perth	Hobart
1851	38	28	28	—	—	—
1861	23	27	28	20	33	28
1871	26	27	27	13	—	25
1881	31	30	33	14	30	23
1891	41	35	37	24	32	22
1901	40	37	39	24	33	20
1911	45	47	41	23	38	21

Source: Table 2 and *Commonwealth Year Books.*

as the spearhead of the frontier. Melbourne contained a large number of recent immigrants, but that is characteristic of a region of recent settlement in the first stage of its development; it gained from the primitive level of development of inland towns that might have shared some of its urban functions, but that reflects the economic organization of the wool-growing industry at that time. Melbourne grew rapidly in the 1850s due to the gold rushes, but alluvial gold mining, compared to wool-growing, created a large demand for labour at the point of production and favoured the growth of country towns near the mining areas, and so reduced Melbourne's share of Victorian population to 23 per cent in 1861.

Melbourne grew more slowly in the 1860s and 1870s, but increased its share of Victorian population to 31 per cent in 1881. In the 1880s the city grew more rapidly, at nearly 6 per cent a year, and this was much faster than the rest of Victoria so that by 1891 four out of ten Victorians lived in the capital. Compared to other cities, however, Melbourne's growth in the 1880s was somewhat less spectacular than is usually thought. So far as rates of growth are concerned, Sydney equalled Melbourne during the decade, and Adelaide had grown faster in the 1870s. Melbourne's share of her colonial population in 1891 was higher than Sydney's by 6 percentage points, but if one considers the Riverina to be part of Melbourne's hinterland–as Melbournians claimed it was–the difference falls to 4 percentage points. Melbourne failed to grow during the 1890s; her modest rate of growth in the 1900s was faster than that of the rest of the state.

Sydney's rate of growth from 1851 to 1891 was high and steady at 5 to 6 per cent, except for the 1860s, and after 1891 population increase was faster and more even than in Melbourne. Sydney's share of her colonial population also grew more evenly. It is not surprising that Sydney took several decades to catch up to Melbourne after the gold rushes, but her sustained growth after 1891 will not be adequately explained until historians cease to be mesmerized by the Melbourne land boom and bank crashes. Melbourne's more irregular growth may be attributed principally to the immediate effect of the gold rushes and to the echo effect on population structure in the 1880s, which was, admittedly, exacerbated by speculative excesses in the late 1880s and the sudden collapse of urban investment in housing and public utilities.[15]

The hypothesis that the capital cities grew in proportion to their hinterlands, thus weakened by Victoria's unusual demographic history, gains in plausibility when we look at the remaining cities. Adelaide's fairly rapid growth up to 1881, then slower but steady growth from 1881 to 1911, reflects the two main phases of South Australia's economic development. For several decades the agricultural, pastoral and mining industries prospered, but by 1881 farming and grazing had reached the limits of occupation and the main copper deposits were exhausted. In the 1880s South Australia lost population as farmers migrated to the Victorian wheat lands and urban workers, thrown out of employment with the depression of the building trades, went to Melbourne. In the three following decades of reconstruction and diversification of rural industries, the population of South Australia outside Adelaide grew at less than 1 per cent a year, while Adelaide grew at about 2 per cent a year. Adelaide's share of South Australian population thus continued to grow after 1881 despite general economic stagnation.

The South Australian turning point from long investment boom to depression, a decade in advance of the eastern mainland colonies, has two implications of general interest. The close correspondence with the main phases of New Zealand's economic growth, due to the similarity of their resources, suggests that one could extend to the Australian regional economies Dr J. A. Dowie's explanation of the inverse relationships of the New Zealand and eastern Australian economies in this period.[16] Second, it was in the 1880s that liberal governments in South Australia began, in response to the social problems created by economic stagnation, to develop policies and legislation on state banking, arbitration, closer settlement schemes and social welfare, which Victorian and New South Wales governments were able to ignore so long

[15] The population aspect of N. G. Butlin's explanation (*Investment . . .*, Chapters III and IV) has been elaborated by A. R. Hall, 'Some Long Period Effects of the Kinked Age Distribution of the Population of Australia 1861-1961', *Economic Record*, Vol. XXXIX (April 1963), pp. 43-52; and by Allen C. Kelley, 'Demographic Cycles and Economic Growth: The Long Swing Reconsidered', *Journal of Economic History*, Vol. XXIX (December 1969), pp. 633-56.

[16] J. A. Dowie, 'Inverse Relations of the Australian and New Zealand Economies, 1871-1900', *Australian Economic Papers*, December 1963, pp. 151-79.

as the boom lasted. Australian historians, looking, as is their wont, only at the latter colonies, have been able to attribute such legislation to the influence of the newly-formed political labour parties, and so establish the notion of parties of initiative and resistance that Professor Henry Mayer has criticized for the twentieth but not the nineteenth century.[17]

Brisbane's rapid rate of growth up to 1891 is due mainly to the lag of Queensland's economic development behind the southern mainland colonies. The pastoral, mining and sugar-growing industries that largely determined the rate of economic growth in Queensland each developed as geographical extensions from the southern colonies; they became important only from the 1860s and, given their geographical distribution, favoured the growth of northern ports and inland mining towns at the expense of Brisbane. Brisbane held one-quarter of Queensland's population by 1891 and then barely managed to retain this share, as sugar-growing in particular continued to move northwards. Hobart also suffered from geographical shifts in rural industries, for economic growth in Tasmania was confined to the west coast mining fields and the northern coastal plain which exported potatoes and other crops to mainland cities. This benefited Launceston rather than Hobart whose immediate hinterland displayed some attempts at diversification but little net growth. There seem to be good reasons why Hobart and Brisbane had considerably smaller shares of their colonial populations than did the larger cities. These reasons would also lead one to expect a similarly small share for Perth, the capital of an almost completely stagnant hinterland until the gold discoveries of the 1890s. A share of one-third throughout the period is therefore surprisingly large.

Why was Perth so large? Why did Adelaide, so much smaller than Melbourne and Sydney, yet contain a comparable share of colonial population? To explain these paradoxes, it is necessary to add two further arguments to an already complex explanation. The third argument, implicit in the staple theory of economic growth and confirmed empirically by Professor Berry, is that land-extensive export industries, especially wool-growing, favour a primate urban distribution; more generally, the less complex the economic structure of the countryside the larger will be the capital city. Victoria met this requirement prior to 1851 and Western Australia prior to 1891 (although the convict establishment in Perth from 1850 to 1870 should be taken into account). Adelaide seems to require a special explanation. It was too small to benefit from 'autonomous' growth as did Melbourne and Sydney, and

[17] H. Mayer, 'Some Conceptions of the Australian Party System, 1910-1950', *Historical Studies*, Vol. VII (November 1956), pp. 253-70.

its relatively complex regional economy, in which wheat and copper were more important than wool, should have favoured the development of country towns. The unique characteristic in South Australia that outweighed these tendencies was the compactness of the hinterland and its accessibility to Adelaide. R. M. Haig in 1926 developed an unusual theoretical model of a spatial economy which assumed that transport was costless; all activities other than agricultural and pastoral then agglomerated in one metropolis because of internal and external economies of scale. 'Instead of explaining why so large a portion of the population is found in urban areas, one must give reasons why the portion is not even greater. The question is changed from "Why live in the city?" to "Why not live in the city?".'[18] It seems likely that the relevant 'transport' costs were lower for Adelaide than for the other Australian cities and that Adelaide was closer, to that extent, to Haig's theory.

'Grand theory' has its uses in giving one a bird's-eye view of the terrain, but it is now time to return to ground. Walks through the six cities would certainly exhaust the modern historian and I have chosen to look only at Melbourne, which was sufficiently large to illustrate the transition from the walking to the public transport city, and, owing to its even topography, displays more clearly than does Sydney the common features of urban expansion in this period.

Some features of Melbourne's later population distribution were already evident in 1851. The City of Melbourne had some 20,000 people while a further 9,000 urban dwellers lived beyond its incorporated limits. Terraces and brick houses had been built on the higher parts of Fitzroy and Richmond adjacent to East Melbourne, and workers' cottages clustered around the butcheries, boiling-down works and small manufactories on the low-lying areas of Richmond and Collingwood. A more dispersed extension had begun to the east and south of the Yarra River, whence city gentlemen commuted from residences in Kew, Prahran, St Kilda and Brighton. A third extension was to the seaports, Williamstown at this time being more important than Port Melbourne.

The large increase of population during the 1850s altered considerably the distribution of population. Although the City population almost doubled to 37,000 in 1861, its share of the total fell to 30 per cent owing to the more rapid growth of population outside the City from 9,000 in 1851 to 88,000 in 1861. The inner suburbs, as defined in Table 4, now held 44 per cent of the total population; those across

[18] R. M. Haig, *Major Factors in Metropolitan Growth and Arrangement*, New York 1927, quoted in E. E. Lampard, 'The History of Cities in Economically Advanced Areas', *Economic Development and Cultural Change*, Vol. III, No. 2 (1955).

the Yarra River to the south and east held 18 per cent and the northern and western suburbs were as yet lightly populated. Of the inner suburbs, Fitzroy was in 1861 mainly a lower middle class residential suburb within walking distance of the City (and so performed a role similar to that of Paddington in Sydney). Seventy per cent of its houses were brick or stone and most were terraces, compared to Collingwood and Richmond, where small wooden cottages outnumbered brick houses by three to one. These suburbs were now distinctly working class areas in which factories and houses intermingled; middle class people seeking home sites jumped them to the more salubrious elevated areas of Kew and Hawthorn to the east of the Yarra River, and to Prahran, St Kilda and Brighton to the south. South Melbourne and Port Melbourne now had over 2,000 wooden cottages, of which three-quarters contained less than five rooms. The residents walked to work in the City or the factories, rope yards and engineering shops located along the Yarra River and near the port. Of the people living outside the inner suburbs, 16,000 lived in Prahran and St Kilda; the remaining 17,000 were scattered in a wide arc around the City from Brighton in the south-east to Williamstown in the south-west.

The distribution of population in 1861 persisted through to 1881. In this period, greater Melbourne doubled its population, but the

Table 4

POPULATION OF MELBOURNE, 1861 TO 1911

Groups of Suburbs	1861		1881		1891		1901		1911	
	000	%	000	%	000	%	000	%	000	%
1. City of Melbourne ...	37	30	66	25	73	15	69	14	71	12
2. Inner suburbs	55	44	122	45	182	39	173	36	188	32
3. South and east	23	18	51	19	120	25	131	28	163	27
4. North and west	10	8	29	11	98	21	105	22	140	24
5. Other areas	—	—	—	—	—	—	—	—	31	5
	125	100	268	100	473	100	478	100	593	100

Source: Appendix and Victorian Censuses.

Notes: The suburbs are grouped as follows: Group 2: Fitzroy, Collingwood, Richmond, North Melbourne, South Melbourne, Port Melbourne. Group 3: Prahran, St Kilda, Brighton, Kew, Hawthorn, Camberwell, Malvern, Caulfield. Group 4: Williamstown, Footscray, Essendon (including Flemington and Kensington), Brunswick, Coburg, Northcote, Preston. Group 5: Shipping in the harbour and areas outside the listed suburbs but within the 10-mile radius. Certain areas are excluded in the earlier years (as explained in the Appendix) until they are considered to be sufficiently urban to warrant inclusion. The annexation in 1905 of North Melbourne and of Flemington and Kensington (previously portion of the City of Essendon) by the City of Melbourne precludes accurate comparison of 1911 with previous years in Groups 1 and 2. The available data has been used to maintain comparability with a maximum error of not more than two per cent for Group 1 and one per cent for Group 2.

City grew more slowly than the rest of Melbourne and its share of total population declined by 5 per cent. One feature of the 1881 distribution, not fully evident in the figures presented in Table 4, is the degree to which Melbourne was still a 'walking city'. The table shows that the City and inner suburbs contained 70 per cent of the total population in 1881; but if Prahran and St Kilda immediately to the south, and Brunswick to the north, are included in the 'walking city' (and Kew and Hawthorn are somewhat arbitrarily omitted) the larger group contained 84 per cent of the population in 1881. The economic and social differentiation evident in 1861 had also sharpened by 1881. Abattoirs, tanneries and other noxious trades located along the Maribyrnong River gave their unique flavour to the Footscray and Flemington area, and South Melbourne and Port Melbourne had attracted industries dependent on the shipping trade. Brunswick had become a working class residential suburb, housing City workers and those employed locally in brickmaking, stone dressing, potteries and hardware manufactures.

The City and inner industrial suburbs now contained 188,000 people living in 37,000 houses, and residential building had to compete with offices, stores, shops and factories for use of land—the scarce factor of production in the inner area of a city. The growing competition for land gradually built up pressure in favour of residential building in the outer suburbs rather than closer in. First, the rising cost of inner City land relative to the cost in other areas would favour residential dispersion of both the working and middle classes, provided that the lower cost of building sites in the outer suburbs was not cancelled out by higher transport costs of getting to and from work in the City. Second, the increasing density of land use in the inner area was beginning to create important social and economic diseconomies for residents. The inner areas now stank from filth and night soil, and were becoming markedly unhealthy to live in, and the spread of factories and other non-residential buildings further reduced their social and economic desirability, despite their greater accessibility to the City. These factors, given a continued increase in population, were the background to the residential expansion of the 1880s, which inaugurated the second main period in the spatial history of Melbourne, as the 'walking city' gave way to the more dispersed 'trains and tramways' city, which was to survive until the 1950s when it began to give way to the automobile city.[19]

Population increase during the 1880s took place almost entirely

[19] The preceding paragraphs are drawn from a lecture given to the Victorian Historical Association and printed in their journal *Historian*, No. 17 (September 1967), pp. 24-31.

outside the city core. The inner suburbs gained 60,000 people and grew at 4 per cent a year for the decade, with Richmond and South Melbourne accommodating half the increase owing to the greater availability of building land. The southern and eastern suburbs gained 69,000, or 9 per cent a year, of which two-thirds was in Hawthorn, Prahran and St Kilda, which had better public transport facilities, and were closer to the City, than new suburbs such as Camberwell and Malvern. The northern and western suburbs also gained 69,000, but grew faster at 13 per cent a year. As with the previous group, the bulk of the increase—70 per cent—took place nearest the City, in Brunswick, Footscray and Essendon, although the rise of manufacturing in these suburbs was also important. Two characteristics of housing that can be documented from the 1891 census indicate the degree of spatial differentiation that had occurred. The first relates to the choice of building materials. The high proportion of four brick or stone houses—most of them terraces—for each wooden house in the City and Fitzroy reflects the relative scarcity of land and the heritage of higher-income housing; the ratio was nearly equal in Collingwood, Richmond and North Melbourne, while in South Melbourne and Port Melbourne wood outnumbered brick by two to one. The southern and eastern suburbs had 12,000 brick and 11,000 wooden houses; the western and northern suburbs had 7,000 brick and 14,000 wooden houses, with very high proportions of wooden houses in Williamstown and Footscray. Data on the size of houses confirms the impression of economic and social differentiation. In the inner suburbs, 56 per cent of the houses had less than five rooms, compared to 26 per cent in the southern and eastern suburbs. The 'new' suburbs of the 1880s expansion, such as Camberwell, Malvern and Caulfield, contained only 16 per cent of small houses.

There can be no doubt that the growth of Melbourne stagnated during the 1890s. Population rose by only 5,000, the number of houses declined from 99,000 to 94,000, and W. A. Sinclair comments on the almost complete depression of the building industry up to 1899.[20] These aggregate figures, especially for the number of houses, are somewhat misleading, for a detailed comparison of the 1891 and 1901 censuses reveals quite an amount of rebuilding within suburbs and groups of suburbs. The inner industrial suburb of Collingwood, for example, suffered a net loss of 866 houses owing to the demolition of small decrepit wooden cottages to make way for new factory buildings; yet the number of brick houses increased by 78, the number of houses with less than five rooms fell by 1,270, and those with more than five rooms

[20] *Economic Recovery in Victoria 1894-1899*, Canberra 1956, pp. 103-4.

rose by 404. This process of rebuilding, which took place mainly in the manufacturing suburbs, can be discerned only by detailed examination. It reflects an important spatial aspect of urban economic growth. Houses are required in certain specific localities, and a geographical shift in the effective demand for houses will itself create new investment despite the existence of vacant houses in other areas of Melbourne. This seems to have occurred, to a minor extent, during the 1890s. The following decade saw a resumption of population growth in which the shift of population towards the new suburbs (somewhat accentuated in Table 4 by the inclusion in 1911 of other areas) continued, so that the share of the City and inner suburbs had now declined from 74 per cent in 1861 to 44 per cent in 1911.

As Melbourne grew in size, its various areas assumed distinct and specialized functions within the whole. The city core, which initially embraced all urban functions, came to specialize in commerce and banking, transport and government, and relinquished other functions, such as housing and noxious industries, to other areas. The inner industrial suburbs had assumed a distinct identity as industrial and working class residential areas and by the 1880s were becoming fully occupied. A second group of industrial suburbs to the north and north-east of the City then grew more rapidly—the noxious trades located in Footscray and Flemington, and the building trades in Brunswick and Northcote. These suburbs also came to house several thousands of workers who commuted to work at City factories, warehouses and shops. The middle class residential suburbs to the east and south of the City broke away from their rural district councils as soon as they could to form municipalities in which residential interests dominated in the local government; they then passed legislation to expel deviant functions such as noxious trades, and discouraged the entry of manufacturing and other activities requiring a large labour force.

The character of each area and its rate of growth can be understood only in relation to its function within the metropolis. As each area became more specialized, and so achieved a distinct identity, it also became more dependent for its functioning on other areas of the City. This was especially true of the middle class residential suburbs, for their growth rested entirely on a typically urban functional specialization between consumption and production. Once people lived in the suburbs and worked in the City, the suburbs had no coherent history—except that of parish pump politics—and can acquire historical meaning only in the wider context of the metropolis. It follows that Australian social historians will have to work out a new methodology for the study of the cities; for the methodology informing the recent excellent social histories of rural regions and towns is inappropriate to the city.

Economic historians have, at present, less of a problem, for their first task must be to study the principal urban industries—manufacturing, trade and finance, residential building—for which there are accepted historical methods and a reasonably adequate kit of analytical tools. The larger problem, that of writing a coherent social and economic history of the Australian cities, remains for the future.

Appendix

POPULATION OF THE CAPITAL CITIES, 1851 TO 1911

This Appendix offers an alternative set of figures to those presented in T. A. Coghlan's *Statistical Account of Australia and New Zealand 1903-4*, p. 155 (the same figures are available in other editions). Coghlan took his figures from the colonial censuses and one can safely assume, as he did, that they are reliable. Each census, however, offered detailed figures that can be combined in various ways to yield different totals depending on one's view of the extent of the urban area at the time; it is Coghlan's choice of figures, and not the figures themselves, that is questioned. An example is that Coghlan chose to exclude the port of Fremantle from Perth's population, so that Perth was the only city to be deprived of its port population. Coghlan may have thought that Fremantle was too distant to justify inclusion (whereas Port Adelaide was not too distant from Adelaide) in the city population; I have included Fremantle to achieve consistency with the other cities, but more importantly because I judge it to be part of the urban complex of Perth as a capital city. A second example is that Coghlan's figures for some cities for the period 1851 to 1871 or 1881 are usually for the city corporation or municipality (the central area of a few square miles) and so excludes 'suburbs', which certainly existed, at least in Melbourne, Sydney, and Adelaide, as early as 1851. For some cities Coghlan then expands his area to the 314 square miles contained within a 10-mile radius of the central point of the city. Although reliable in the sense that they were calculated by the colonial statisticians from detailed census returns, the 10-mile figures overstate urban population relative to the pre-1881 figures, and also absolutely, as contemporary maps and local histories show that much of the area remained rural as late as 1911. My attempt to define an expanding urban area is outlined below.

Table A-1

MELBOURNE (thousands)

Year	Coghlan	McCarty
1851	23	29
1861	140	125
1871	207	191
1881	283	268
1891	491	473
1901	494	478
1911	—	593

Coghlan's 1851 figure is for the City of Melbourne (including Fitzroy which became a separate municipality in 1858). It is too low because Richmond and Collingwood were 'thriving suburbs' and Brighton, a residential suburb, and Williamstown, the main port, were well established in 1851 (Serle, *The Golden Age*, p. 3). Bate has a figure of 2,000 for Brighton but this includes market gardeners and farmers (*History of Brighton*, p. 71). The County of Bourke, excluding the City of Melbourne, held 18,348 people, of which I estimate 6,000 as urban, making 29,000 for 'greater' Melbourne. Coghlan's figures for 1861 to 1901 are the official 10-mile figures. They are too high especially in the earlier years. For 1861 and 1871 I have excluded the following areas: (a) the statistical divisions that later became the municipalities of Camberwell, Malvern, and Caulfield; (b) Coburg, Northcote, and Preston to the north of the City; and (c) the remaining large peripheral belt of unincorporated land. This contracts greater Melbourne to an area within a 5-mile limit (except for Brighton which was established just outside the limit) and reduces the area of the City from 314 to about 80 square miles. So sparsely settled was the outer 5-mile zone in 1861, however, that this revision reduces the urban population by only 15,000 from Coghlan's figure.

In the 1870s and 1880s suburbs spread into some of the areas just excluded, and I take account of this as follows: in 1881, half the population of (a) and (b) is included; in 1891 and 1901 all of (a) and (b) is included but (c) remains excluded; in 1911 (c) is included. These changes are based on the evidences of increasing density of local statistical areas, and on local histories that often contain quite detailed information on the transition from rural to suburban functions: in addition to Blainey and Bate see W. G. Swift, *History of Northcote* (1928), J. B. Cooper, *History of Malvern* (1935), I. Southall, *A Tale of Box Hill* (1957); and contemporary handbooks and gazetteers such as R. P. Whitworth, *Official Handbook . . .* (1880). The main safeguard against error in changing the urban boundaries in this way is that the outer zone contained relatively few people. In 1901, for example, the area (c) above accounted for about half the area but only 4 per cent of the population inside the 10-mile limit.

Table A-2

SYDNEY (thousands)

Year	Coghlan	McCarty
1851	54	54
1861	96	96
1871	138	138
1881	225	225
1891	383	400
1901	488	496
1911	—	648

Coghlan uses census figures for an area that grew from census to census as successive portions of the urban fringe achieved municipal status and were then added by the Statistician to the population of greater Sydney. The expanding boundary overstates urban population in so far as newly-incorporated areas contained rural population for some time after their incorporation; on the other hand the country surrounding Sydney was infertile and did not support a large farming population. Coghlan pointed out that Sydney's population of 383,000 in 1891 was contained within an area of only 120 square miles, compared to Melbourne's 256 square miles (with a population of 491,000), and claimed—rather patriotically so far as can be judged from the figures—that by using the larger area he could increase Sydney's population to 440,000 (*Wealth and Progress of N.S.W.*, 1892, p. 745). The area used in 1911 was 185 square miles. I accept Coghlan's figures for 1851 to 1881, but revise those for 1891 to 1901 (and the 1911 census figure of 636,000) by adding to them the populations of the municipalities of Granville, Auburn, and Rookwood. These municipalities comprised flat, swampy land 8 to 10 miles west of Sydney and immediately to the east of Parramatta; unattractive to residential builders, the land was cheap and located on a railway and so attracted manufacturers in the 1880s. In this decade the Clyde Engineering Works (employing 800 hands in 1890), Brunton's Flour Mills, Hudson Bros timber-yards and other manufacturers shifted from cramped inner-city sites to Granville and Auburn, and others followed in later decades. Details are available in a series of articles in the *Evening News* (1891), bound together in the Mitchell Library collection of Newspaper Cuttings, Vol. 159.

Coghlan's figures for 1851 and 1861 are for the Corporation of Adelaide. They are clearly too low, for as early as 1851 middle class

Table A-3

ADELAIDE (thousands)

Year	Coghlan	McCarty
1851	15	18
1861	18	35
1871	43	51
1881	104	92
1891	133	117
1901	162	141
1911	—	169

people were living in Kensington and Norwood to the east and in Unley to the south of the Corporation, and factories and workers' cottages were located lower down the Torrens River (to the west) in Hindmarsh. Coghlan's 1871 figure lies between that of the Corporation of Adelaide (27,208) and my estimate of the population contained within a 10-mile radius (60,379), but no combination of detailed census figures can be made to match Coghlan's figure. For 1881 to 1901 Coghlan uses the Statistician's figures for the 10-mile radius, but these are too high, as most of the land lying between 4 and 10 miles from the centre of the City was rural until well into the twentieth century. The South Australian Statistician was a keen user of this definition of the urban area, perhaps because Adelaide, relative to other Australian capital cities, had a dense adjoining population of farmers, orchardists, and market gardeners to the east and south. The density of this rural population increases the possible degree of error in attempting to calculate an expanding urban area; and frequent changes in statistical boundaries throughout the period are a further difficulty. For these reasons, and also to illustrate the arbitrariness of my estimates, it may help to explain, more fully than for the other cities, the methods adopted. The figures are presented in Table A-4.

(i) The total population of the Corporation of Adelaide is included throughout, despite the existence of vacant blocks in the 1850s and 1860s. The unsuccessful attempts of the Corporation to increase the rates on these blocks is described in T. Worsnop, *History of the City of Adelaide* (Adelaide 1878).

(ii) During the 1880s and 1890s the Corporation of Port Adelaide absorbed large portions of neighbouring district councils. This reflected the growth of urban population associated with the port, and suggests that an expanding urban area for Port Adelaide should be defined, but an attempt to do so was frustrated by numerous boundary changes. I therefore take the area within the 1901 boundary (this remained unchanged in 1911) and calculate its population back to 1861. My figures therefore overstate population especially in the early period but this is negligible as the rural areas adjoining the port were sandy and swampy and contained few people. For details of boundary changes see the *Centenary History . . . of Port Adelaide* (Adelaide 1956).

Table A-4

POPULATION OF ADELAIDE, 1861 TO 1911

	1861	1871	1881	1891	1901	1911
Corporation of Adelaide	18,303	27,208	38,479	37,837	39,240	42,294
North of Torrens River						
Port Adelaide	3,176	5,287	13,922	17,140	20,089	24,015
Woodville and Hindmarsh	3,309	4,473	8,399	11,546	15,575	19,122
Yatala and Prospect	1,151	1,234	1,879	3,812	5,271	6,813
Walkerville	600	674	1,419	2,101	2,962	3,595
South of Torrens River						
West Torrens and Thebarton	673	736	1,465	3,827	5,304	8,720
St Peters and Payneham	1,160	1,700	3,803	7,036	9,440	11,415
Kensington and Norwood	3,386	5,132	10,087	11,747	12,568	13,892
Burnside	1,210	1,557	3,370	6,185	7,773	9,416
Unley and Mitcham	1,704	1,778	5,493	11,429	18,152	23,773
Glenelg and Brighton	708	1,324	3,495	4,524	5,029	6,110
TOTALS	35,380	51,103	91,811	117,184	141,403	169,165

(iii) Woodville district council was a large triangle of land to the north-west of the Corporation of Adelaide, bounded on the south by the Torrens River, on the west by the coast and on the north-east by a line drawn between Adelaide and Port Adelaide. The land was sandy and unattractive to farmers, and the great bulk of the population, which grew from three thousand in 1861 to 19,000 in 1911, lived in the industrial working class suburb of Hindmarsh and along the railway line between Adelaide and Port Adelaide. Official statistics do not permit a precise location of farming and manufacturing activities in Woodville, but literary evidence supports my decision to include the total population throughout (and so overstate slightly the true urban population): K. R. Bowes, *The 1890 Maritime Strike in South Australia* (MA thesis, University of Adelaide, 1957), Chapter 1. South of the Torrens River the industrial working class suburb of Thebarton was an extension of Hindmarsh; administratively it formed part of West Torrens district council until its severance in 1883. I include half the population of West Torrens 1861 to 1881, then the total population of Thebarton 1891 to 1911, thus excluding any 'urban' population in West Torrens from 1891, and perhaps compensating for the element of over-estimation in Woodville in the same period.

(iv) Across the Torrens River to the north of Adelaide, Prospect and Walkerville grew only slowly as residential suburbs. Walkerville district council had constant boundaries from 1861 and is included from that year. Prospect district council is included from 1881; prior to that year Prospect formed the southern tip of the larger Yatala district council, and I have extrapolated backwards the 1881 ratio of population in Prospect and Yatala to obtain urban figures for 1861 and 1871.

(v) To the east of Adelaide, I define a constant area comprising the Corporation of St Peters (created in 1883) and Payneham district council and include this from 1861. To obtain a figure for 1861 I assumed that half the population of Payneham district council was urban. In excluding Campbelltown district council throughout I understate urban population in this sector, but Campbelltown had only 1,333 people in 1871 and 2,342 in 1911. Immediately to the south of St Peters-Payneham, and due east of Adelaide, lay the populous middle class residential suburb of Kensington and Norwood, which is included from 1861 onwards and presents no definitional problems. Its suburban character is fully documented in G. W. Gooden and T. L. Moore, *Fifty Years' History of the Town of Kensington and Norwood* (Adelaide 1903). The suburb grew rapidly during the 1870s, and, with the aid of horse tramways, housing spread eastward into Burnside district council, whose population trebled between 1881 and 1911. A growing proportion of Burnside's population was urban; lacking detailed information to estimate the proportion, I include all Burnside as urban and hope that the cumulative list of over- and under-estimates may cancel each other.

(vi) South of Adelaide, Unley Corporation (which ceded from Mitcham district council in 1871) was a large middle class suburb, whose total population is included from 1881 when separate figures become available. For 1861 and 1871 I assume, after reading W. A. Norman's *History of the City of Mitcham* (Adelaide 1953), that half the population of Mitcham was urban. Some portion of Mitcham's population after the severance of Unley in 1871 was urban, but is excluded. There remain the seaside suburbs of Brighton and Glenelg. Prior to the 1850s Glenelg, 6 miles south-west of Adelaide, had rivalled Port Adelaide as the main port, but large vessels had to ride anchor well out from shore. Mails continued to be unloaded at Glenelg until 1888 but cargo had been confined to Port Adelaide since the 1860s. Until the opening of a private railway from Adelaide in 1873, Glenelg, having no manufactures and very little in the way of agriculture, relied on the port for its livelihood and for this reason its total population is included from 1861 onwards. It attracted some commuters after the opening of the railway but held only 4,000 people at the turn of the century. Its local history contains useful detail for the urban historian: W. H. Jeanes, *Glenelg . . .* (Adelaide 1956). South of Glenelg, the village of Brighton catered for neighbouring farmers and, in summer, Sunday trippers to the beach. An important local industry after 1880 was lime and cement manufacture using local limestone. I exclude Brighton until 1881, when it then changes suddenly and completely from a rural village to an urban annex of Adelaide.

Table A-5

BRISBANE (thousands)

Year	Coghlan	McCarty
1851	3	3
1861	6	6
1871	15	15
1881	31	31
1891	94	87
1901	119	92
1911	—	117

Coghlan's figures for 1851 to 1861 are for the town portions of the police districts of North and South Brisbane, Fortitude Valley and Kangaroo Point. The 1871 to 1881 figures are for the census district of Brisbane, which apparently covers the same area as the portions of the police districts, for a table in the 1871 census compared directly to the 1871 and 1861 figures. The 1871 figure is the smallest of several quoted in the 1871 census: a central (undefined) area of eight and three-quarter square miles had a population of 18,455, and an area called 'Brisbane and suburbs' had 19,413. Maps and literary sources (especially Greenwood and Laverty, *Brisbane 1859-1959*, Brisbane 1959) suggest that the 1851 to 1861 figures are correct but that the 1871 to 1881 figures are too low owing to the rise of new if still sparsely settled suburbs. Attempts to define a larger area for these years were frustrated by lack of detailed figures and the intermingling of suburban residents with sugar-growing and other agricultural population that was characteristic of the Brisbane urban fringe. I therefore have to accept Coghlan's figures. Coghlan's 1891 figure is the Queensland Statistician's calculation for a 5-mile radius, and his 1901 figure is for a 10-mile radius. Both areas are too large at this stage of Brisbane's development, and I have calculated for the period 1891 to 1911 an expanding area that as late as 1911 is smaller than that within the 5-mile limit.

1891: the census districts of Brisbane, Enoggera, Toowong, and half of those portions of Caboolture, Oxley and Moreton East that lie within the 5-mile limit.

1901 and 1911: the districts of Brisbane, South Brisbane, Windsor, Hamilton, Ithica, Toowong, Taringa, Coorparoo, and Stephens, as defined in the 1911 Commonwealth Census. I have thus excluded the marine resorts of Wynnum and Manly 20 miles east of Brisbane, and Sandgate 13 miles north of Brisbane, even though Sandgate was connected with Brisbane by rail in 1882 and in 1897 one authority wrote that it 'is in fact regarded largely as a suburban residential locality' (J. J. Knight, *Brisbane*, 1897, pp. 71-2).

Table A-6

PERTH (thousands)

Year	Coghlan	McCarty
1851	—	—
1861	—	5
1871	5	—
1881	6	9
1891	8	16
1901	36	61
1911	—	107

Coghlan's figures are clearly inconsistent. His 1871 and 1881 figures are for the Perth census district, which is too large an area for those years. His 1891 figure, for the much smaller area of the City of Perth, is too low as it omits suburbs that had developed by this time. For 1901 Coghlan rejected the official estimate of 66,832 for the 10-mile radius (but accepted that definition for Brisbane in 1901) and chose a smaller area that comprised Perth, Subiaco, Leederville, Victoria Park, North Perth, and South Perth (1901 Census, Vol. I, p. 93). He excluded Fremantle, 12 miles distant from Perth, in all years. My inclusion of Fremantle in all years produces substantial differences between Coghlan's and my figures. My 1861 figure is the sum of the 1859 census figures for the towns of Perth and Fremantle. For 1871 there are no figures available for areas smaller than the Perth census district (5,244) which Coghlan used: the Perth and Fremantle census districts yield the high figure of 9,040. To estimate some figure smaller than 9,040 is more than usually dangerous as the cessation of transportation caused sudden population changes in the years around 1871. The growth rate for Perth-Fremantle, 1861 to 1881, is based on the census district figures and so assumes a constant relation between the urban and rural populations of the districts. My 1881 figure is for Perth and Fremantle municipalities, and my 1891 figure is for the two municipalities plus two statistical subdistricts that were not predominantly urban (the area remains smaller than for the two census districts of Perth and Fremantle). Perth-Fremantle grew rapidly in the 1890s as a result of the gold rushes and the following new suburbs are included in the 1901 figures: Subiaco, Leederville, Victoria Park, South and North Perth, South and North Fremantle, Claremont, and Cottesloe. In 1911 Midland Junction and Guildford, 10 miles up the Swan River from Perth, are included for the first time. Guildford, one of the earliest towns in the colony, served as the market centre for the Swan district until the rise of Midland Junction intercepted its trade with settlers on the eastern side of the river, and limited its hinterland to the West Swan district. It was the trans-shipment point for goods from the Eastern Districts which went by river boat to Fremantle and remained a village until early in this century. Contemporary sources around 1900 referred to it as a town or village, rather than a suburb. Midland Junction developed around the junction of the Midland Railway Company's line with the state system, and became a market town. In 1905, the government railway workshops were moved from Fremantle to Midland Junction, and this strengthened the links between Midland Junction and Perth and Fremantle.

Table A-7

HOBART (thousands)

Year	Coghlan	McCarty
1851	—	—
1861	19	25
1871	19	26
1881	21	27
1891	33	33
1901	35	35
1911	—	40

Coghlan's figures for 1861 to 1881 are for the City of Hobart (an area of 2 square miles) and so exclude immediately adjoining areas that were at least partly urban in these years. The *Australian Handbook* (1878) says that Newtown, a mile to the north of Hobart, 'is so connected by buildings as to appear a suburb of that city', and describes Sandy Bay and Bellerine as suburbs. Coghlan's figures for 1891 to 1901 are for the City plus the adjoining municipal districts of Queenborough, Newtown, and Glenorchy. I have used the larger area for the period of 1861 to 1911.

R. V. JACKSON

OWNER-OCCUPATION OF HOUSES IN SYDNEY, 1871 TO 1891

It has long been accepted that in nineteenth-century Australia a high proportion of new housing was built for owner-occupation rather than for rental. As early as the 1850s, W. S. Jevons was writing of the Sydney suburb of Redfern: 'Almost every labourer & mechanic here has his own residence on freehold or leasehold land & unpretending as it is to any conveniences or beauties, it yet satisfies him better than the brick built, closely packed & rented houses of English towns.'[1] More recently, N. G. Butlin has suggested that owner-occupiers accounted for well over half of total Australian housing in 1891.[2] The present exercise does not question this proposition. Rather, it attempts to investigate one source of variation in the incidence of owner-occupation between different areas within Australia as a whole. Here, the starting point is the census of 1911, which provided for the first time aggregate information on the numbers of owner-occupied and tenanted houses. The census data show that almost exactly half the occupied houses in Australia were owner-occupied in 1911. However, this aggregate figure conceals an important difference between the experience of the capital cities, on the one hand, and the rest of Australia, on the other. In the six state capitals only 36 per cent of occupied houses were occupied by owners or instalment-purchasers. In non-metropolitan areas the corresponding figure was 57 per cent. In each capital city tenanted houses outnumbered those occupied by their owners, whilst the reverse was the case in non-metropolitan areas in each state. The difference between the incidence of owner-occupation in the capital city and in the rest of the state was greatest in Victoria. In 1911 owner-occupiers accounted for 35 per cent of occupied houses in Melbourne and 62 per cent of occupied houses in the remainder of the state. Among the mainland states, the gap was smallest in Queensland, where owner-occupiers accounted for 47 per cent of occupied

[1] W. S. Jevons, 'Remarks on the Social Map of Sydney', p. 28; original manuscript in the Mitchell Library in Sydney, bound with 'A Social Survey of Australian Cities, 1858'.

[2] N. G. Butlin, *Investment in Australian Economic Development, 1861-1900*, Cambridge 1964, pp. 259-60. See also pp. 212, 222 and 275-8.

houses in the metropolis and 62 per cent of occupied houses in non-metropolitan areas.

The question is whether the relatively low share of owner-occupation in metropolitan housing evident in 1911 also characterized the experience of the capital cities in the nineteenth century. Section I presents data for Sydney which suggests that in one capital city, at least, the incidence of owner-occupation was lower than it was at the aggregate level in the period ending in 1891. This is not conclusive evidence, but it is consistent with the proposition that the metropolitan/non-metropolitan contrast that existed in 1911 was also present to some degree in the latter part of the nineteenth century. Sections II to IV constitute a tentative explanation of the relatively low level of owner-occupation in Sydney in the period to 1891. This explanation is conducted in terms of contrasts between Sydney and non-metropolitan New South Wales. Implicit in the explanation, therefore, is the proposition that Sydney's experience in this respect was part of a more general process in which owner-occupiers were relatively less numerous in the capital cities than they were in the rest of Australia. If further research were to show that this was not the case, but that Sydney's experience with respect to the level of owner-occupation was exceptional, the explanation suggested below would need to be modified.

I

In 1911, according to the census data, 31 per cent of the occupied houses in Sydney were owner-occupied, 66 per cent tenanted and the remainder were returned as 'other and unspecified methods of occupancy'. The lack of similar aggregate data on the level of owner-occupation in the nineteenth century forces one to rely on more detailed sources of information. Particularly useful here are the *Assessment Books* compiled by municipal councils for rating purposes.[3] Among other things, council *Assessment Books* record the name of the owner (and/or lessee) and occupier of every unit of ratable property in a particular municipality. Where the name of the occupier of a house is the same as the name of the owner (or lessee), one can safely assume that the house in question was owner-occupied at the time the *Assessment Book* was compiled. Conversely, where these names differ one can assume that the house was tenanted. Using this information, it is possible to build up house by house an estimate of the incidence of owner-

[3] Municipal *Assessment Books* and some of the research uses to which they might be put are described in some detail in P. Balmford and J. L. O'Brien, 'Dating Houses in Victoria', *Historical Studies: Australia and New Zealand*, Vol. 9, No. 36 (May 1961), pp. 379-95.

occupation at a particular date for any area for which *Assessment Books* are available.

The *Assessment Book* data have been used to derive estimates of the relative importance of owner-occupied and tenanted houses in several parts of Sydney in 1891 (Table 1). These estimates refer only to private dwellings and not to structures used by their principal occupants for business as well as residential purposes. Thus combined shops and dwellings, hotels, boarding houses and similar types of residences have been excluded where possible, even though these structures are counted as habitations in the census. The detailed nature of the data meant that estimates of the incidence of owner-occupation could be made for only one date if a significantly large area was to be covered. In this connection, 1891 is a useful date. By then the major phase of metropolitan house building of the 1880s was over, whilst the depression of the 1890s had probably not yet begun to affect the pattern of house ownership. In addition, it is useful to have estimates for a date close to that of the 1891 census, which was the first New South Wales census for some time to contain detailed information upon metropolitan housing. The census was taken in April 1891. The municipal assessments on which Table 1 is based were made at about the same time and probably reflect the position towards the end of 1890 or early in 1891.

The areas included in Table 1 have been placed into five categories. The areas in each category are assumed to be representative of part of the metropolis. For this purpose, Sydney has been divided in the following way.

(1) Residential parts of the municipality of the City of Sydney, represented in Table 1 by Chippendale, Darlinghurst-Potts Point and Surry Hills. The latter areas accounted for about 40 per cent of the City's inhabited dwellings in 1891 and perhaps 60 per cent of the population growth that took place in the City of Sydney during 1871 to 1891. (An area's share in total population growth during 1871 to 1891 is taken as an indicator of its share in house building during that period. This course is dictated by the paucity of the data on metropolitan dwellings in the 1871 and 1881 censuses.) Chippendale was a closely built low-income area south-west of the city centre. Darlinghurst-Potts Point occupied a fashionable ridge east of the city centre. Surry Hills lay between these areas, both geographically and in terms of the social standing of most of its inhabitants.

(2) Areas that were sometimes relatively thinly populated in 1871 but that had been converted into densely populated inner suburbs by 1891. Darlington, Glebe, Glebe Point, Macdonaldtown, Newtown and Paddington represent these areas in Table 1. Also included in this category

Table 1

Owner-occupied and Tenanted Private Dwelling Houses, Selected Sydney Suburbs, 1891

	Occupied private dwelling houses					
	Owner-occupied		*Tenanted*		*Total*	
	No.	%	No.	%	No.	%
City						
Chippendale (a)	109	10	958	90	1,067	100
Darlinghurst-Potts Point (b)	187	17	944	83	1,131	100
Surry Hills (c)	643	14	3,870	86	4,513	100
Inner areas						
Darlington	128	22	460	78	588	100
Glebe (d)	303	16	1,639	84	1,942	100
Glebe Point (e)	263	27	695	73	958	100
Macdonaldtown	248	25	757	75	1,005	100
Newtown	899	29	2,160	71	3,059	100
Paddington	712	23	2,429	77	3,141	100
Southern industrial						
Waterloo	397	26	1,135	74	1,532	100
Medium density						
Ashfield	933	48	1,021	52	1,954	100
Burwood	416	40	621	60	1,037	100
North Sydney (f)	866	33	1,758	67	2,624	100
Randwick	415	49	438	51	853	100
Waverley	602	41	866	59	1,468	100
Outer areas						
Drummoyne	160	64	91	36	251	100
Five Dock	103	59	71	41	174	100
Hurstville (g)	129	58	93	42	222	100
Lane Cove (h)	117	63	68	37	185	100
Willoughby (i)	177	52	161	48	338	100

Notes:

(a) That part of Phillip Ward, City, bounded by the present Broadway, City Road, Cleveland Street and Regent Street.
(b) That part of Fitzroy Ward, City, east of and including Victoria Street and Darlinghurst Road.
(c) Cook Ward, City.
(d) Bishopthorpe, Forest Lodge and Outer Wards, Glebe.
(e) Inner Ward, Glebe.
(f) Belmore, Kirribilli, Tunks, Victoria and Warringa Wards, North Sydney.
(g) 1892. Hurstville and Peakhurst Wards, Hurstville.
(h) Lane Cove Ward, Willoughby.
(i) Chatsworth and Middle Harbour Wards, Willoughby.

Source: Derived from the *Assessment Books* of the Municipalities of the City of Sydney (1891), Ashfield, Burwood, Darlington, Drummoyne, Five Dock, Glebe, Macdonaldtown, Newtown, North Sydney, Paddington, Randwick, Waterloo, Waverley, Willoughby (all 1891-2) and Hurstville (1892-3).

are the municipalities of Balmain, Camperdown and Redfern. The inner areas included in the table held 55 per cent of the group's inhabited dwellings in 1891 and accounted for 56 per cent of the group's population growth during 1871 to 1891. The areas in the table ranged from the top (Glebe Point) to the bottom (Macdonaldtown) of the social scale, though most were predominantly lower middle class or fairly respectable low-income areas.

(3) The southern industrial suburbs, whose pattern of development was unlike that of any other part of Sydney. Table 1 includes only Waterloo from this group of suburbs. Also in the group are the municipalities of Alexandria and St Peters. In 1891, 41 per cent of the group's inhabited dwellings were in Waterloo. The share of the latter in the group's population growth during 1871 to 1891 was 39 per cent.

(4) Areas that were growing rapidly during the 1870s and 1880s but that did not achieve the status of inner suburbs during this period. Ashfield, Burwood, North Sydney, Randwick and Waverley represent this group of suburbs in Table 1. The balance of the group is the municipalities of Leichhardt, Marrickville, Petersham and Woollahra. The areas in the table contained 47 per cent of the group's inhabited dwellings in 1891 and accounted for a similar percentage of the group's population growth during 1871 to 1891. Like the medium density suburbs in general, the representatives of this group in the table (and particularly Ashfield) contained large areas of above-average housing.

(5) The outer suburbs, comprising all the metropolitan area (as defined in the 1891 census) not included in one of the above categories. Drummoyne, Five Dock, Hurstville, Lane Cove, and Willoughby represent the outer suburbs in Table 1. The areas included in the table held just under 20 per cent of the inhabited dwellings in the outer suburbs in 1891 and accounted for a similar proportion of the group's population growth during 1871 to 1891. The choice of areas in Table 1 was determined partly by the desire to include suburbs ranging across most of the social scale.

The data in Table 1 suggest that well under half of Sydney's houses were owner-occupied in 1891. If each of the five parts of the metropolitan area distinguished above is given a weight corresponding to its share in the stock of inhabited metropolitan dwellings recorded in the 1891 census, the figures in Table 1 imply that 30 per cent of inhabited metropolitan dwellings were owner-occupied at that date. The precise figure is not to be taken literally, for the experience of each group of areas in Table 1 may not be fully representative of those parts of Sydney to which it has been applied. However, even if this figure of 30 per cent does understate the share of owner-occupied in total dwellings (and there is no presumption that any bias in the data is in this direction), the scope for bias can scarcely be sufficiently large to endanger the proposition that by 1891 a substantial majority of Sydney's houses were tenanted rather than owner-occupied.

The data in Table 1 also permit somewhat more tentative inferences to be made about the pattern of new building in Sydney during the period ending in 1891. These inferences rest on the assumption that the share of owner-occupied houses in the stock of dwellings in a particular area in 1891 equalled the share of owner-occupation in new building in that area during 1871 to 1891. There is, of course, no *a priori* reason why this should have been so. Nevertheless, this condition does appear to have been satisfied reasonably well in each of the three areas in Table 1 for which estimates have been made of the share of owner-occupation in new building in the period up to 1891 (see Table 2). These areas are Glebe Point, Macdonaldtown, and Paddington. In Paddington, 23 per cent of occupied houses were owner-occupied in 1891. The share of owner-occupied in new houses built during 1871 to 1891 was 25 per cent. In Glebe Point and Macdonaldtown the share of owner-occupied in total housing in 1891 was 27 per cent and 25 per cent respectively. During 1876 to 1891 the share of owner-occupied in new housing was 25 per cent in each of these suburbs. In each of these three areas, the fairly close correspondence between the share of owner-occupation in the stock of housing in 1891, on the one hand, and the share of owner-occupation in new building in the period up to 1891, on the other, was the result of two offsetting developments. The first of these was a fall over time in the share of owner-occupation in new building which means that, other things being equal, the 1891 stock figure will overstate the share of owner-occupation in new building in the preceding period. This was offset by a small net tendency for the level of owner-occupation of existing houses to fall over time as changes occurred in the pattern of ownership and occupation of these houses.

Given this, it seems reasonable to assume that the stock figures for particular suburbs in 1891 can serve as a rough guide to the pattern of building in these suburbs in the preceding period. On this assumption, and weighting each group of suburbs in Table 1 by its share in metropolitan population growth, the data in the table suggest that 33 per cent of new houses built in Sydney during 1871 to 1891 were owner-occupied. Again, the precise figure is not to be taken literally. However, it does seem clear that significantly less than half of the houses built in Sydney during this period were built by or for owner-occupiers. Most of the houses built in Sydney during 1871 to 1891 are likely to have been owned by landlords rather than by their occupiers and the typical occupier of new housing is likely to have been a tenant.

If, as is generally believed, owner-occupation did account for over half of total housing and new building in Australia as a whole in the period ending in 1891, it does seem from Table 1 that Sydney differed significantly from this general pattern. Whether Sydney was the sole exception to the general pattern is not clear and cannot be determined until detailed work has been done on other areas. In the following section an attempt is made to explain the low level of owner-occupation in Sydney in terms of contrasts between metropolitan and non-metropolitan New South Wales. Thus the argument proceeds as if Sydney's experience with respect to the level of owner-occupation was in some degree characteristic of the Australian capital cities in the nineteenth century. Given the metropolitan/non-metropolitan contrast evident in the 1911 census data, and given the similarity in the share of owner-occupied in total dwellings in Sydney in 1891 and 1911, this is a reasonable working hypothesis. However, it remains no more than this until detailed work has been done on the other Australian capitals.

II

It may be useful to approach the question of the low level of owner-occupation in Sydney initially by way of N. G. Butlin's analysis of the conditions underlying the high level of owner-occupation in Australia as a whole in the period up to 1888. If it can be shown that some or all of these conditions were less typical of metropolitan than they were of non-metropolitan areas, this may go some way towards explaining the low level of owner-occupation in Sydney, whilst still remaining within the general framework of Butlin's analysis. Butlin isolates three factors that are said to have combined to produce a situation favourable to building for owner-occupation. These factors are (1) a high level of rents (2) low house construction costs in relation to wage incomes and (3) a high level of employment and high rate of population growth.[4] Leaving aside the last of these as being at least as applicable to metropolitan as to non-metropolitan areas, there remain two factors that are said to have favoured building for owner-occupation: high rents and low construction costs in relation to average wages.

It would be difficult to argue that rents tended, on average, to be lower in Sydney than in non-metropolitan New South Wales in the period to 1891. On the contrary, rents in the metropolis were probably significantly higher than elsewhere in the colony. Thus, if high rents did stimulate building for owner-occupation rather than for rental, as Butlin appears to contend, owner-occupation should have been more

[4] N. G. Butlin, op. cit., pp. 275-8.

rather than less common in Sydney than in the rest of the colony. However, it is not perfectly clear what Butlin has in mind here. The obvious interpretation of Butlin's argument is that, from the occupier's viewpoint, high rents made tenancy relatively dearer and hence relatively less attractive than home ownership. But it can be argued that, given the prospective rate of return upon alternative investment opportunities, high rents are just as likely to have stimulated building for rental through their favourable effect upon the prospective rate of return upon capital invested in tenant houses. It it not clear why high rents should not have stimulated investment by would-be landlords at least as much as investment by would-be owner-occupiers. Until more is known about the framework in which high rents occurred, there is little hope of determining their probable effect upon the level of owner-occupation. In these circumstances, and in the present state of knowledge, it is not possible to decide whether higher rents in the metropolis can help explain the lower incidence of owner-occupation in that area or whether, on balance, the high level of metropolitan rents actually militated against the establishment of a low level of owner-occupation in Sydney.

The way in which construction costs affected the incidence of owner-occupation is perhaps more interesting. Low construction costs in relation to wage incomes can be said to have encouraged building for owner-occupation to the extent that they made it possible for most of the population to own their own home. It is important to note the exact nature of the figures used in this connection. Butlin says: '*Excluding land purchase*, the cost of a standard four-roomed *weatherboard* house rarely exceeded twice the annual wage income and, in fact, fluctuated between 1½ and 2 times the average wage income.'[5] If one is concerned with eastern Australia as a whole, or even with New South Wales as a whole, it is correct to use the cost of building a *weatherboard* house as an indicator of average housing costs. In New South Wales as a whole well over half the residential rooms added during 1871 to 1891 were weatherboard. But the typical material used in house building differed between metropolitan and non-metropolitan New South Wales. During 1871 to 1891 weatherboard rooms accounted for four-fifths of residential rooms added in non-metropolitan New South Wales. In Sydney, however, only one-fifth of rooms added during this period were weatherboard and four-fifths brick.[6] Thus the correct procedure is to relate the construction costs of *brick* houses to wages when dealing with Sydney and to relate the construction costs of

[5] Ibid., p. 277. Italics not in original.

[6] N. G. Butlin, *Australian Domestic Product, Investment and Foreign Borrowing, 1861-1938/39*, Cambridge 1962, p. 259.

weatherboard houses to wages when dealing with the rest of the colony. The point is that during this period construction costs per room appear to have been half as much again for brick as opposed to weatherboard houses.[7] Hence, if construction costs of a four-roomed weatherboard house were twice annual wage incomes, construction costs of a four-roomed brick house would be three times annual wage incomes. To the extent that brick houses were typical of the metropolis and weatherboard houses typical of the rest of the colony, therefore, and assuming wage rates to have been much the same throughout the colony, the barriers to individual home ownership may be said to have been significantly higher in Sydney than they were in non-metropolitan New South Wales.[8]

At this stage it is convenient to introduce a related factor that is deliberately neglected by Butlin, with some justification in a national context, but which is important when comparing different areas within Australia as a whole. This factor is the price of building land. Land prices were considerably higher in Sydney than in the rest of New South Wales. Whilst it is difficult to be precise about comparative land values, the gulf between metropolitan and non-metropolitan land prices was so wide that absolute precision is not necessary. Perusal of details of a large number of sales of building allotments suggests that in 1880, before the metropolitan land boom had begun to get out of hand, the buyer of a reasonably placed 15 ft to 20 ft allotment in any of the suburbs where the majority of metropolitan house building was taking place would have been lucky if he paid no more than £5 per foot; whilst in most country towns the seller of a well positioned half-acre lot would have been lucky to get as much as £5 for the whole allotment.[9] Thus site values were probably a negligible factor in the cost of non-metropolitan housing but were high enough to add substantially to the cost of metropolitan housing. This meant that relatively high land prices in Sydney reinforced any effect that higher construction costs may have had upon the level of owner-occupation in the metropolis.

[7] Ibid., p. 257.

[8] It might be objected that, for comparable dwellings, building costs might have been lower in Sydney than in rural areas, thus offsetting the effect of the differential incidence of brick houses upon relative building costs. However, N. G. Butlin's figures suggest that in Victoria urban and rural weatherboard construction costs tended to be much the same during 1871 to 1891. Moreover, Butlin's Victorian figures suggest that average brick construction costs were at least 20 per cent *higher* in urban than in rural areas. Butlin notes that the margin between urban and rural building costs was probably narrower in New South Wales than in Victoria. Ibid., pp. 254-7.

[9] These prices are based upon the sales records of the Sydney real property auctioneers, Richardson and Wrench. The firm's *Contract Books* for the period 1858-1936 are in the Mitchell Library in Sydney.

A hypothetical example may serve to set this matter in perspective. Butlin's estimates of construction costs suggests that in New South Wales it may have cost an average of about £75 per room to build a brick house and about £50 a room to build a weatherboard house during 1871 to 1891. According to the census data, the typical house built during this period contained five rooms. Thus the normal metropolitan brick house may have cost about £375 to build and the typical non-metropolitan weatherboard house may have cost about £250. Land costs did not increase the latter figure significantly. However, the cost of land would have added at least £75 to £100 and often considerably more to the cost of most metropolitan houses occupying a single building allotment. As a rough approximation, therefore, the average metropolitan house built upon a single allotment may have cost almost twice as much as its non-metropolitan counterpart, if land costs are taken into account. In other words, it is not unreasonable to assume that the barriers to individual home ownership, as represented by the cost of house purchase, may have been almost twice as high in Sydney as they were in the rest of New South Wales in the period up to 1891.

Why should the higher cost of metropolitan housing have limited building for owner-occupation *more* than building for rental? Should not higher construction costs and higher land prices have discouraged rental investment to the same extent as they discouraged investment for owner-occupation? Butlin does not spell out his reasons for believing that the level of construction costs affected rental investment in a fashion different from investment for owner-occupation. However, at least two reasons may be advanced to support the notion that dearer housing in Sydney tended to reduce the relative importance of building for owner-occupation.

First, the nature of the restraint imposed upon would-be owner-occupiers by high construction costs and high land prices may have differed from the nature of the restraint that high unit costs imposed upon would-be landlords. It is central to Butlin's analysis that the would-be owner-occupier's desire to own his own home was little affected by direct market considerations. In particular, rates of return upon alternative investment opportunities were probably largely irrelevant, within wide limits, to decisions about buying one's own home. High costs of home ownership did not operate principally upon an individual's *desire* to own his own home but upon his *ability* to do so. The higher the cost of home ownership, the smaller the proportion of people able to afford it. With landlords the effect of high unit costs probably operated in a different fashion. For most landlords, the effect of high unit costs upon the ability to invest was probably less important than the effect upon prospective returns. Given rent levels, higher unit costs meant lower returns per unit of capital invested. But rent levels were generally higher in Sydney than in the rest of New South Wales, a circumstance that in part actually reflected the better quality of metropolitan housing (in terms of materials employed) and the higher price of metropolitan land. Thus the adverse effect of higher unit costs upon building for rental was probably largely offset by the fact that potential returns were also higher in Sydney. To this extent, higher unit costs can be expected to have had a proportionately smaller adverse effect upon building for rental than upon building for owner-occupation.

Second, metropolitan landlords who built two or more adjoining houses were able to cut unit costs in a way that was not normally open to would-be owner-occupiers. Two savings available to landlords but not to owner-occupiers can usefully be distinguished. The first related to construction costs. Significant economies in unit cost almost certainly resulted from devices such as the use of party walls and common chimneys serving two adjoining houses in a terrace. The second saving related to land costs. Would-be owner-occupiers generally had no option but to put one house on one block of land, whilst terrace houses almost invariably occupied less than one building allotment each. Sometimes, two houses were squeezed onto a single allotment. More often, three houses were accommodated upon two allotments or four or five houses upon three allotments. The total savings upon unit costs involved here could be fairly large. There is at present no way of knowing precisely the extent of the economies in physical construction costs involved in the building of terraces as against detached houses. However, some rough calculations can be made to show the scope for reducing land costs through the erection of terraces. During the early 1880s, when most building in Sydney took place, 15 ft allotments in the inner suburbs were being sold for an average of perhaps £10 a foot. Thus for a detached house on a single allotment land costs may have amounted to about £150. Placing three houses on two adjoining allotments would have reduced this figure to £100 per house. Would-be owner-occupiers could share these savings to the extent that terraces that had been erected by speculators were sold in broken lots to individual occupiers. However, the *Assessment Books* of the municipalities included in Table 1 suggest that this practice was uncommon. The sales records of the Sydney firm of real property auctioneers, Richardson and Wrench, also suggest that it was usual to dispose of speculators' terraces in one line.

It should be noted that landlords outside Sydney probably had a much smaller cost advantage over non-metropolitan owner-occupiers. Where land was very cheap, as it was in most parts of non-metropolitan

New South Wales, there was little scope for reducing land costs through the erection of terraces. Further, in a situation where most people were content to live in wooden rather than brick houses there was little point in constructing terraces. Construction costs of wooden terraces were probably little cheaper than those of detached wooden houses and brick terraces were probably dearer than any sort of wooden house. On the whole, therefore, it is not likely that unit costs were generally significantly lower for landlords than for owner-occupiers in non-metropolitan areas.

III

If there is anything in this analysis of the reasons for the low level of owner-occupation in Sydney as a whole, it should be capable of being applied also to variations in the incidence of owner-occupation between different parts of Sydney. In other words, a high proportion of brick houses and high land prices might be expected to have characterized those parts of Sydney where the level of owner-occupation was lowest. There is some evidence to suggest that the proportion of brick houses in different parts of Sydney varied directly with population density. If the 36 municipalities in the Sydney metropolitan area are ranked on the basis of (1) population density and (2) the share of brick and stone in total dwellings in 1891, Kendall's co-efficient of rank correlation is 0.65, significant at the 1 per cent level. Population density itself tended to fall as distance from the city increased. Further, other things being equal, suburban land prices can be expected to have varied directly with population density and inversely with distance from the city, with distance defined to take account of available transport routes and facilities. In these circumstances, it may not be going too far to suggest that the closer a suburb was to the city, the more densely it had been built up, the higher were its land values and the higher was the proportion of brick to wooden houses—in short, the more thoroughly *urban* was an area's character—the smaller was the role of the owner-occupier likely to be.

The figures in Table 1 appear to fit this analysis reasonably well. The case is clearest at the extremes. Owner-occupation was clearly most important in the outer suburbs, which were still sparsely settled in 1891. Land prices here were low. Even at the height of the land boom of the 1880s, good 30 ft to 50 ft allotments in the outer suburbs were freely available at £1 to £2 a foot. In none of the outer suburbs included in Table 1 did the share of brick and stone houses in total dwellings exceed 60 per cent.[10] Owner-occupation was least important

[10] *Census of New South Wales*, 1891.

in Chippendale and Surry Hills, almost adjacent to the main business area. There was little vacant land in either of these areas by 1891. In 1885, 20 ft to 25 ft allotments on the outer limits of Surry Hills were being sold for £12.5*s* to £23.10*s* a foot.[11] In the 1891 *Assessment Book* only land on the outskirts of Surry Hills and Chippendale, or land away from the main thoroughfares, was valued at less than £15 a foot. In 1891 well over 90 per cent of the houses in both areas were built of brick or stone.[12] The analysis can accommodate finer gradations than this. Inspection of Table 1 reveals a rising level of owner-occupation as one moves from the city through the inner areas and industrial suburbs to the medium density areas and finally the outer suburbs. This visual impression is confirmed by rank correlation analysis. It is not possible at present to rank accurately the areas in Table 1 on the basis of land values or distance from the city (as defined above), but firm rankings can be made on the basis of population density and the share of brick and stone houses in total dwellings. If the areas in Table 1 are ranked on the basis of (1) the share of tenanted houses in total dwellings and (2) population density in 1891, Kendall's co-efficient of rank correlation is 0.77, significant at the 1 per cent level. Ranking these areas on the basis of the share of (1) tenanted houses and (2) brick and stone houses in total dwellings in 1891 produces a rank correlation co-efficient of 0.73, again significant at the 1 per cent level.

These correlation co-efficients would be higher were it not for the experience of a handful of suburbs where the level of owner-occupation differed fairly sharply from that suggested by their population density and by the quality of their dwellings, in terms of materials employed. In particular, the share of owner-occupied in total dwellings was significantly lower in Waterloo and significantly higher in Ashfield, Drummoyne and Glebe Point than population density and the incidence of brick and stone houses in these areas might have led one to expect. In each case, this appears to have been related to the social standing of the area in question. Waterloo was thoroughly working class, whilst Ashfield, Drummoyne and Glebe Point were fashionable areas in 1891. Thus it seems that, other things being equal, the level of owner-occupation varied directly with the social standing of the various parts of Sydney. The social standing of an area was probably of some importance in determining land prices and the incidence of 'superior' building materials in a particular area, but its influence on the level of owner-occupation probably ran counter to the influence of the latter variables.

[11] Richardson and Wrench, *Contract Book* 33 (old firm).
[12] *Census of New South Wales*, 1891.

The modifying influence of the social standing of different suburbs is consistent with the analysis developed above. The importance of high construction costs and high land prices is that they made housing dear in relation to the means of would-be owner-occupiers. So far it has been assumed that there were no regional variations in the average income and wealth of the population. In the context of a discussion of metropolitan and non-metropolitan contrasts, this assumption is probably justified. But in the context of a single city it is clear that some areas will be socially much more desirable than others and that, on the whole, the inhabitants of these more desirable areas will tend to be wealthier than the inhabitants of other parts of the city. Therefore, a larger proportion of the population of better class areas may be expected to have been able to afford their own homes at a given level of construction costs and land prices. This implies some modification of the pattern of owner-occupation that one would expect to have been associated with the latter variables.

Nevertheless, the modifying influence of the social standing of the different parts of Sydney was important only at the margin. The most fashionable area dealt with in Table 1 was Darlinghurst-Potts Point, where owner-occupation was still less important in 1891 than it was in most of the low-income suburbs covered by the table. Indeed, the incidence of owner-occupation was half as high again in the least fashionable areas in Table 1 (Waterloo and Macdonaldtown) as it was in Darlinghurst-Potts Point. By this time land prices in the Darlinghurst-Potts Point area had gone so high as to prevent even the moderately wealthy from owning their own houses. As early as 1871 land in Darlinghurst was fetching up to £7.10*s* a foot at auction.[13] In 1882, 18 ft to 20 ft allotments fronting narrow back streets were sold for £10 to £29 per foot.[14] The 1891 *Assessment Book* valued vacant land in Darlinghurst-Potts Point at an average of £25 to £30 a foot, with £50 a foot being not uncommon in the more exclusive parts of the area.

IV

The trend of the above discussion suggests that a low level of owner-occupation was more characteristic of densely populated inner suburbs than of the more sparsely populated outlying parts of Sydney during the late nineteenth century. Hence the relative importance of building for owner-occupation in any area might be expected to have fallen progressively as that area was built up. In order to check whether this was so, information is needed upon the pattern of ownership and

[13] Richardson and Wrench, *Contract Book* 14 (old firm).
[14] Richardson and Wrench, *Contract Book* 28 (old firm).

occupation of new houses built in a particular area during the period in which that area was being transformed from a sparsely populated outer suburb to a densely populated inner suburb. Here municipal *Assessment Books* are again a valuable source of information, for they enable one to identify new houses as they were built and provide data on the pattern of ownership and occupation of these houses. New houses built in a particular area during any period can be identified by comparing the *Assessment Books* referring to the beginning and end of that period. In practice, the comparison of entries in successive *Assessment Books* is a tedious and often difficult process,[15] particularly as street numbering was not generally introduced until late in a suburb's development. Changes in the ownership of existing houses often makes it difficult to identify them in later *Assessment Books.* The demolition of old houses also presents a number of problems. Despite these difficulties, however, it is possible in most cases where *Assessment Books* have survived to derive a substantially accurate list of houses built during a particular period. Analysis of the names of owners and occupiers recorded for these houses in the later *Assessment Book* will then give the pattern of ownership and occupation at the end of a particular period of houses built during that period. This is not precisely the same thing as the pattern of ownership and occupation of new houses in that houses built during the early part of a period may have changed hands before its close, but the approximation is close enough for most purposes.

Table 2 contains estimates of the level of owner-occupation of new houses built in successive 5-year periods in three Sydney suburbs—Paddington for 1871 to 1901 and Macdonaldtown and Glebe Point for 1876-91. These estimates were derived by comparing *Assessment Books* covering these areas and dated at 5-year intervals. The detailed nature of the *Assessment Book* data precluded treatment of more than a few small areas. However, the choice of areas in Table 2 is appropriate, for each area was sparsely populated in the early 1870s and had been well built up by the early 1890s. Moreover, these areas ranged over the whole social scale: Macdonaldtown was largely working class, Paddington lower middle class and Glebe Point upper middle class throughout the period.

The experience of each of the suburbs dealt with in Table 2 appears to have been roughly what the analysis developed above would lead one to expect. In 1871-6, owner-occupiers accounted for 43 per cent of new houses built in Paddington. By 1881-6 this figure had fallen to 17 per cent. Similar though less spectacular falls in the relative

[15] On this see P. Balmford and J. L. O'Brien, loc. cit.

Table 2

LEVEL OF OWNER-OCCUPATION OF NEW PRIVATE DWELLING HOUSES, SELECTED SYDNEY SUBURBS, 1871 TO 1901

	Private dwelling houses built in each 5-year period					
	Owner-occupied at end of period		*Not owner-occupied at end of period*		*Total*	
	No.	%	No.	%	No.	%
Glebe Point (a)						
1876-81	75	31	166	69	241	100
1881-6	103	23	336	77	439	100
1886-91	51	23	171	77	222	100
Macdonaldtown						
1876-81	78	34	149	66	227	100
1881-6	112	21	421	79	533	100
1886-91	47	23	156	77	203	100
Paddington						
1871-6	116	43	154	57	270	100
1876-81	263	32	552	68	815	100
1881-6	197	17	930	83	1,127	100
1886-91	114	19	488	81	602	100
1891-6	41	11	327	89	368	100
1896-1901	29	9	308	91	337	100

Note: (a) Inner Ward, Glebe.

Source: Derived from the *Assessment Books* of the Municipalities of Glebe, Macdonaldtown (1876-7 to 1891-2) and Paddington (1871-2 to 1901-2).

importance of building for owner-occupation occurred in both Macdonaldtown and Glebe Point. The pattern evident in Table 2 is consistent enough to suggest that there may indeed have been a strong tendency for the relative importance of building for owner-occupation in a particular suburb to fall as the development of that suburb proceeded.

Not all of the fall in the relative importance of owner-occupation in the areas covered by Table 2 was due simply to the fact that they were being converted from outlying areas to thickly populated suburbs. Part of the decline in building for owner-occupation as development proceeded was attributed above to the associated rise in land prices. But in the period up to 1885 rising land prices in Macdonaldtown, Paddington, and Glebe Point were a compound of two elements. The first element is the important one for the above analysis—the tendency for the price of land to increase *relative* to land prices in areas not being developed in a similar fashion. In other words, the price of land shifted away from the low level appropriate to an outer suburb and towards the higher level appropriate to a densely populated inner suburb. The second element was an upward shift in the whole structure of metropolitan land prices in the period up to 1885. This reinforced the price increases in the areas covered by Table 2. Hence, before 1885, it may be that owner-occupation declined further than was implied simply by the transformation of these areas to densely populated inner suburbs. This may help explain the slight tendency for the relative importance of building for owner-occupation in the areas dealt with in the table to rise again in the second half of the 1880s, when land prices in Sydney as a whole tended to fall. The relative position of these areas did not worsen, but land prices there nonetheless sagged because of a downward shift in the whole structure of metropolitan land prices.

One final point here concerns the experience of Paddington in the 1890s. By this time, new building for owner-occupation in Paddington appears to have dwindled to very low levels. There is at present no way of telling whether this decline in building for owner-occupation was typical of Sydney as a whole in the 1890s. What does seem clear, however, is that the events of the 1890s are not likely to be capable of being handled within the framework of the analysis developed above. This analysis has been designed to apply to the period of rapid and more or less sustained expansion in income and employment up to the end of the 1880s. The disruption of income and employment associated with severe depression, the curtailment of building finance flowing through building companies and societies and the reduced scale of total building in the 1890s constituted so large a disturbance as to make it unlikely that the analysis developed above can be applied to this decade in precisely the same way as it has been applied to the period before 1891.

Australian National University

M. J. KELLY

EIGHT ACRES: ESTATE SUB-DIVISION AND THE BUILDING PROCESS, PADDINGTON, 1875 TO 1890

The Municipality of Paddington in the near-eastern suburbs of Sydney was one of the areas which experienced rapid population growth in the second half of the nineteenth century. The population of the municipality increased seven-fold between 1861 and 1891, from 2,692 to 18,392. The number of houses increased by the same proportion and the number of rooms nine-fold. Within the 30 years the municipality had grown from a sprawling and distant village into a fully built-up and highly integrated urban community. A detailed examination of the characteristics of the urban development of the municipality, with particular reference to the sub-division of the Good Hope Estate, may help to throw some light on the complex process of Sydney's urban growth in this period.[1]

I

Within these 30 years most of Paddington was sub-divided and developed for residential occupation. The division of large parcels of land began earlier than 1860 and extended well into the twentieth century. But by 1890 seven-eighths of the total 400 acres had been sub-divided in some form and the suburb had assumed its modern form. Furthermore, the activities of the sub-divider as well as the builder had reached a peak in the period 1880-5 when over 1,000 new dwelling houses were added to accommodate over 4,000 new inhabitants. Land prices, which had risen only slightly throughout the first half of the period, accelerated rapidly in the period of active speculation and development (1875-85) and by 1890 a marked change had occurred in the nature of house tenure as well as in the rents paid for tenanted houses.

Before 1873 the activities of the sub-divider, although noticeable, had yet to result in any marked change in the physical landscape. Whereas there had been a total of 95 assessments for vacant land-

[1] Unless otherwise stated all data used has been taken from Municipality of Paddington *Assessment Books* held by the Sydney City Council at the Paddington Town Hall for the relevant municipal year (beginning the first Tuesday in February).

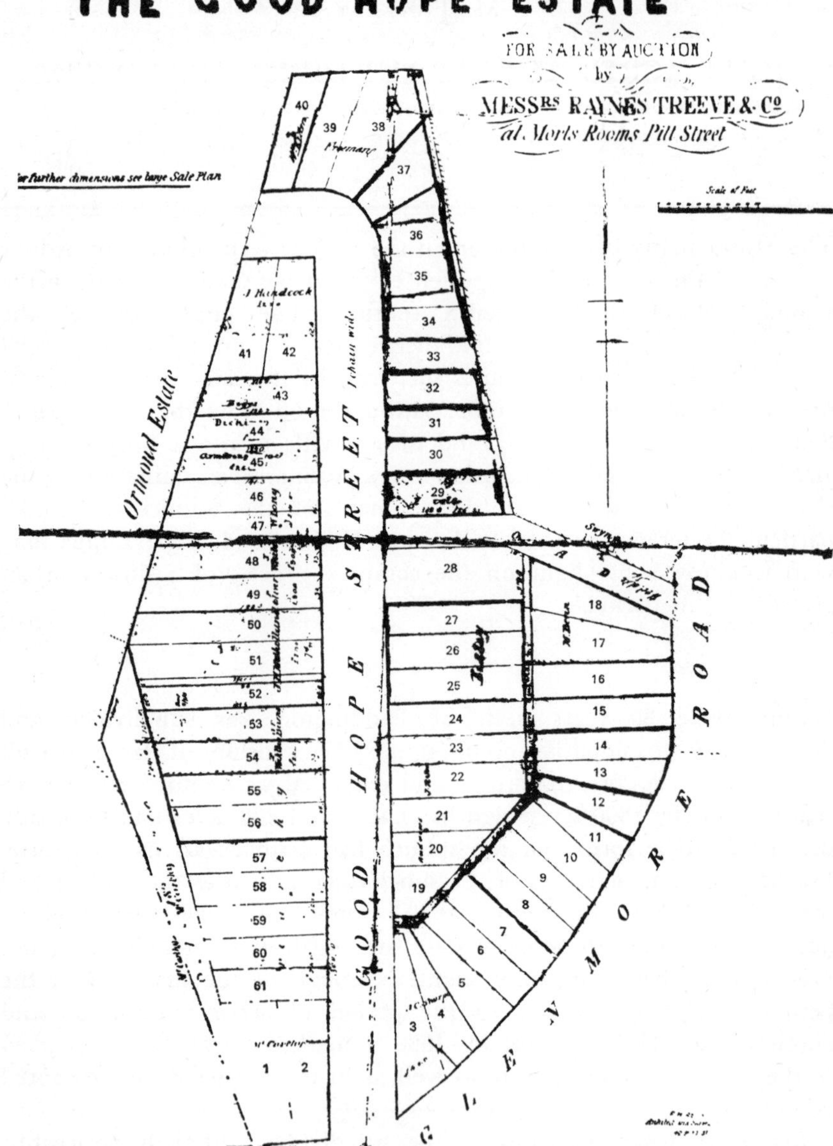

THE GOOD HOPE ESTATE

This plan is a copy of the original prepared for the auctioneers and from which lithographs were prepared for pre-sale distribution. Allotment numbers have been superimposed. (From the original in the Mitchell Library)

owners in 1863 (17 of whom held about 90 per cent of vacant land) in 1873 there were 234 land assessments; 92 per cent of these were of land with an estimated capital value of between £40 and £80 and with a total estimated capital value of £10,980. The remaining 20 land-owners between them held land with a total capital value of £19,580. In short the large land-owner holdings still dominated the small.

The 90-acre Underwood Estate existed much as it had done in 1863. But whereas it had then been given an annual valuation of £2,234, the gross capital valuation had risen to £10,900 one decade later. Rates payable (calculated at 5 per cent of capital value) had thereby increased from £111.14*s* to £545. This five-fold increase in rateable values, a function of the increasing concern by aldermen to equate rateable values with real prices and strengthen municipal finance was common throughout the suburb. Those owners of estates[2] which were to become prominent as sub-divisions in the 1870s—the Holdsworths, I. F. Halle, Mrs Booth, the MacDonald Estate, Edward Hill, W. Taylor and W. Perry, the Underwood and Olive Bank Estates—faced rapidly increasing rate charges.

The pressures encouraging land sub-division were, therefore, becoming increasingly diverse. Not only was the increase in land prices generally (and particularly City of Sydney land prices) forcing a suburban spread. Not only was population increase causing new pressures on domestic housing facilities at a time when the demand for commercial land in the city was causing a change in usage of Sydney buildings from dwellings to shop and office. There was also the significant factor of increasing cost, in terms of rising rateable values, to the suburban land-holder. For Paddington, it was these owners of vacant land who were the most anxious to sub-divide. Their property-owning counterparts who lived on the estate were to prove the most reluctant to participate in sub-division. Those land-owners who lived other than on the estate were the first to divide; those who had a more personal interest, the 'gentlemen' inhabitants, were the last. Even when land prices were rising most rapidly in the early 1880s there were still a number of resolutes unwilling to forego the family estate.

This latter group of men were nonetheless atypical. Between 1874 and 1880, 910 allotments were offered at *initial* sub-division (the majority of these being further sub-divided as the building process gathered momentum). Within this 7-year period, five of Paddington's most substantial land-holdings, accounting for some 30 per cent of the

[2] 'Land-owners' here are distinct from those owner-occupiers whose houses were set in large estates. There was little change in 'the gentry' sector throughout the decade. Any change that did occur was, in the short term at least, towards consolidation of estates rather than to sub-division.

total area, were put up for auction. One of these, the Good Hope Estate, was offered by Messrs Raynes Treeve & Co. at Morts Rooms, Pitt Street, in May 1875.

The subsequent development of this estate can be included in the Paddington and Sydney-wide process of speculative house building to take advantage of rental opportunities throughout the 1880s.[3] Such a simple description does, however, obscure the role played by the small-scale owner-occupier (often also a builder-occupier) in the building of the estate.

II

The Good Hope Estate was described as an area which

> enjoys one uninterrupted view of unsurpassed grandeur, . . . grassy slopes and oceans of woodlands, the ornate grounds of the neighbourhood properties, and the villas of Darling Point—while the background is relieved by the waters of our lovely harbour, with its bold rocky points and headlands, all of which lend enchantment to the view, and form a picture of artistic beauty rarely if ever excelled.[4]

The land itself did not fall far short of its advertised advantages. The 'oceans of woodland' consisted of tea-tree, native gum and scrub land which bordered on the well-cultivated gardens and orchards of the neighbouring Glenmore Road *élite*. Glenmore Road housed the prosperous professional class with their servants, stables, handsome gardens, splendid wells and unpretentious mansions. The Good Hope Estate was thus accorded, by the auctioneer at least, a degree of social distinction. It was seen 'as a site for a Mansion or for a Terrace of first class residences'[5] since it was an area 'superior to any and within but a comfortable walk to the heart of the commercial area of the city'. Furthermore, it was claimed that Paddington had become 'the most important and rapidly advancing suburb in our city'.[6] The new suburb was not only 'healthful' owing to its elevated position but also offered 'grand and spectacular views'. In addition the estate offered the possibility of neighbours of the class of W. J. McCarthy of Deepdene House and Alderman J. E. Begg living only slightly further afield in the gracious and imposing Olive Bank Villa.

The eight-acre estate, originally a Crown grant to Richard Hoddle in 1833, was put up for auction on account of the trustees of the MacDonald Estate. MacDonald, a large estate owner in the area, had bought

[3] See R. V. Jackson's essay.
[4] Richardson and Wrench, *Contract Book* (old firm), May 1880, Mitchell Library.
[5] Ibid., May 1878.
[6] Ibid.

the original Hoddle grant in 1861 for £200.[7] He was described as one of those 'old identities of the Paddington area' who had 'passed away to "the great majority"'[8] thereby allowing his descendants to realize upon their legacy.

Over 70 per cent of the estate was sold on the day of auction. By 1877 only 9 per cent of the original 61 allotments remained with the estate trustees.[9] By 1891 67 houses with an annual estimated rental value of £2,238 had been erected on the 45 original lots which it has been possible for me to examine in detail.[10]

Upon sub-division the area (exactly 8 acres 2 roods 0 perches) was sub-divided into 61 lots, based around Good Hope Street which was to be 1 chain wide (see map). The majority of lots fronting the street were given a 33-ft frontage. Where lots could not be given a 'sufficient' depth (between 140 ft and 160 ft) a compensating increase was allowed to the street frontage. The increasing scarcity of vacant land on the estate and the estimated values of land remaining vacant are shown in Table 1. The early 1880s was the period of most pronounced speculative activity in terms of prices and changes of land ownership. This is the only aspect of the development of the estate that could be described as having any of the characteristics of a 'mania'.

Table 1

VACANT LAND, GOOD HOPE ESTATE, 1875 TO 1891

	1875	1879	1883	1887	1891
Footage	908	917	398	339	235
Total capital value (£)	2,240	3,990	2,660	2,620	1,920
Mean capital value per ft (£) (all lots less Lots 1 and 2)	2.5	4.4	6.7	7.7	8.2

Note: The assumption made is that the estimated capital value placed upon land by the municipal authority, as shown in the municipal *Assessment Books*, correctly approximates the real capital value. The *Assessment Book* entries have thus been used to isolate the increase in land values over the period. The correlation between actual prices paid and municipal estimates for the same parcel of land on sub-divisions other than the Good Hope (and for which actual prices paid were obtainable) is sufficiently exact to allow this procedure. Lots 1 and 2 have been excluded because they were probably purchased for commercial purposes.

[7] Municipality of Paddington *Assessment Books*, 1861-3.

[8] *The Illustrated Sydney News*, 10 October 1884.

[9] See plan of sub-division of the Good Hope Estate.

[10] The original sub-division shows 61 allotments. Information concerning 16 of these is not available since the evaluator over the years used no recognizable house-to-house pattern. Thus whilst it is possible to collect rate book data for Good Hope Street (it being wholly included in the estate) it is impossible for Glenmore Road, only a fraction of which is included in the estate. The following analysis will therefore be confined to 45 lots which together constitute Good Hope Street.

Of the 22 original purchasers of the 45 lots, 8 bought 29 lots. William McCarthy, living at Deepdene House, the handsome mansion lying immediately to the south of the Good Hope Estate, bought the lots adjoining his already large estate (Lots 56-61) for £304. In addition McCarthy paid the highest price obtained at the auction, £6.10*s* per ft frontage, for Lots 1 and 2, which since they cornered both the important Glenmore Road as well as Good Hope Street were seen as fine land for commercial use. McCarthy's purchases not only added to his already considerable land-holding in the area, but also enlarged the acreage of the Deepdene Estate which was offered for sale as a sub-division 5 years later.

The only other purchase on a similar scale was one by Maguire who bought nine 33-ft allotments. Otherwise the small purchase was the order of the day—groups of two lots here, three there, with ten purchases by individuals of single lots. For the next few years, and certainly to 1880, change in the pattern of vacant land-ownership was rapid. Only 14 of the original 45 lots did not change hands at least once before houses were built upon them. This suggests that most of the original purchases were for speculative purposes.

Maguire re-sold within the year. His initial investment of £640[11] in 1875 netted him a profit of 20 per cent upon re-sale to Stephen Whelan, a Paddington landlord who bought to build, and to J. Cole, himself a speculator who re-sold to George Davidson, a local stonemason. Maguire retained one of his original allotments (Lot 28) and built a three-roomed cottage for himself and his wife. By the late 1880s the cottage had become the property of Mrs Maguire who managed to sell off her backyard (which faced Hoddle Street) and upon which, by 1890, had been built a further five tiny terraces houses.

Mr Mulholland, the original purchaser of high-land Lots 50, 51 and 52, sold under some pressure[12] 5 years later to Samuel Slade for an annual money appreciation of 31 per cent.[13] Slade in turn re-sold in 1882 to W. H. Lumsdaine, a future 'Boarding Establishment' proprietor, for a capital appreciation on his original outlay of a further 30 per cent for the 2 years. (Lumsdaine's boarding house which was built in 1886 is one of the few original houses not still standing on the Good Hope Estate.) Equally as fortunate as Slade was Thomas Fisher,

[11] Calculated using an average of actual prices obtained for similar lots nearby and estimated capital values for his particular purchases, Lots 28-36 *Assessment Books*, 1875-7.

[12] On 9 May, Richardson and Wrench offered these lots 'overlooking romantic Barcom Glen and on account of the mortgagee'. Richardson and Wrench, *Contract Book* (old firm), A4525.

[13] Ibid., A4527.

the original purchaser of Lots 3 and 4. His property which had cost £440 in 1875 was put up for auction by Richardson and Wrench on 23 August 1878. It was believed that 'on the opening up of Begg Street (through the nearby Olive Bank Estate) and Broughton Street (immediately opposite and which will connect with upper Paddington, Woollahra etc.) it will be the most valuable business corner in this fashionable suburb'.[14] Inducements such as these were clearly insufficient. The property was passed in. Undaunted Fisher almost immediately sold the back portion of Lots 3 and 4 to provide two new building blocks each with a 45-ft frontage to Good Hope Street. The cash forthcoming from this happy venture was presumably sufficient to forestall further sale until 19 August 1880 when Richardson and Wrench sold the by now smaller property to William Hart at an average price of £7 per ft—giving Fisher a 12 per cent annual rate of return.

Overall, the first round of re-sale saw 7 lots (of the 29 lots held by speculators identified earlier) bought by a second round of speculators, themselves buying land only to re-sell within the space of a few years. It was this group of 'second round' speculators who realized the greater capital gain. By 1879 land values in Paddington were appreciating at their most rapid rate. The original speculators had at best doubled their investment over 4 years; the second round speculators achieved this in half the time.

III

After 1880 speculation in land subsided and residential building gathered momentum. Most land purchases on the Good Hope Estate in 1880 and 1881 were by builders and Paddington began to take shape as a suburb. Streets were laid down and old streets were re-aligned. By 1885 three-quarters of the total land area of the Good Hope Estate had completed or near completed houses built upon it.

Except where financial pressure seems to have forced some further sub-division of the original purchase, the land speculator re-sold his original holding as he had bought it. There were only three cases where lots were further sub-divided before re-sale. It was left to the future developer, in particular the builder, to further sub-divide. At the end of the period 79 individual lots (house or land) had been created from the initial 45 lots. Normally, two houses were built upon one original 33-ft allotment. On the Good Hope Estate 23 of these allotments became 46 houses; six allotments became thirteen houses: 29 of the 45 original sub-divisions thus supported 59 terrace houses. Further, two allotments became five houses and five retained their original

[14] Ibid., 23 August 1878.

boundaries. Lot 1 and 2 combined, which became part of the Deepdene Estate, were further sub-divided into eight lots. The most exploited lot was Lot 28. The Maguire cottage was demolished in the 1890s in order to make way for five further terrace houses, each 12 ft wide. Maguire's original purchase then, in 1876, of an allotment 63 ft by 140 ft and costing £158, supported 10 terrace houses which were given an annual rental value of £40 each by 1890. Such was the scope for the ambitious developer. Yet for the Good Hope Estate (as well as for the whole Paddington area) such activity was rare. There is little evidence that the profit motive outweighed all other considerations. The average width of Good Hope Street houses was 16 ft 6in; 59 of a total of 67 houses by 1891 were of this width, a reasonable size for a terrace house.

By 1877, 2 years after initial sub-division, four houses had been erected on the estate, of which two were owner-occupied, and two rented. Table 2 indicates the rapid change that occurred in the period 1879 to 1891. Only two of the total of twelve houses built by 1879 were tenant-occupied. However, 4 years later tenants were occupying some 63 per cent of the 43 occupied dwellings. By 1887 the proportion was similar (64 per cent of a total of 50 houses). In 1891 76 per cent of a total of 67 houses were tenanted rather than owner-occupied. That the majority of the houses on the Good Hope Estate were built for *eventual* letting is clear. Yet the trend established by Table 2 obscures one important facet of the growth of this particular estate from vacant land to tenanted houses. The point is best illustrated by an analysis of the men who built them.

In 1878 Henry Stockham, a builder,[15] bought Lot 57 from McCarthy

Table 2

ESTIMATED ANNUAL RENTAL VALUES ON GOOD HOPE ESTATE

	1879	1883	1887	1891
Houses, owner-occupied				
Number	10	16	18	16
Total annual value (£)	417	781	847	757
Estimated mean annual value (£)	41.7	49.1	47.1	47.3
Houses, tenanted				
Number	2	27	32	51
Estimated total annual value (£)	100	1,361	2,102	2,238
Estimated mean annual value (£)	50	50.6	65.7	43.9

Source: Municipality of Paddington *Assessment Books.*

15 All data concerning occupation groupings of estate personnel have been derived from: (1) *Sands Sydney Directory*, 1879-80, 1882-3, 1884-91; (2) Municipality of Paddington *Land Tax Assessment Book* in Paddington Town Hall. (This book is undated but is most likely a composite transcript of a number of earlier land tax assessments.)

and immediately built a house for himself upon half of the 33-ft allotment. It was 2 years after moving in that Stockham had completed building a second house on the remaining half of the original lot. This house remained tenanted for the remainder of the period, with Stockham as landlord. By 1881 and obviously by now well accustomed to the role of landlord, Henry Stockham bought the 33 ft Lot 21 as well as half (16 ft) of Lot 22. By 1883 the three terraces erected by him on his newly acquired land were all tenanted and remained so (with one brief lapse when the middle house of the three was 'vacant' when the assessor called) at least until 1891.

J. D. Ward, classified as a carpenter in 1881 and as a builder in 1885, followed a similar although slightly less acquisitive path. In 1880 he bought one-third of the 50 ft Lot 19 as well as a half of the 33 ft Lot 20. Upon this land he built two single-storey cottages—one to be owner-occupied, one to be let. George Davidson, by trade a stonemason and working as a contractor-builder, purchased Lots 35 and 36 from the land speculator J. Cole in 1879. Two identical terrace houses were built upon Lot 35, thereby giving each a frontage of 16 ft. The first of these completed by 1879 was occupied by the Davidson family for a period of 3 years. By this time, 1882, Davidson had completed the building of the second (identical) house as well as a more modest third house adjoining. This third house was in fact 'hung' from the external side wall of his second house thereby affording him significant savings in construction costs. Upon completion of this, his final house, the family moved in—enabling him to rent the more imposing pair of houses next door. This he did until 1889 when he moved into what is now number 75 Good Hope Street, the only one of his three houses that he had not as yet lived in. Davidson's plan to further extend his property holdings (by building upon the remainder of his Lot 36) was aborted by a Council decision to construct an extension of Lawson Street connecting it with Glenmore Road. Much of the remainder of Lot 36 together with the whole of Lot 37 were thereby appropriated for that purpose.

Edward Freeman, an original purchaser of Lots 38 and 39, had built what must have been a reasonably modest cottage by 1876. He was a coachbuilder and used the remainder of his holding to carry on his trade until 1888 when he too built (or had built) a second house which remained tenanted to 1891. Lot 48 was originally purchased by J. White, a timber merchant. By 1880 White had entered into some form of partnership with Peter Coghill. As 'contractors and builders' the partnership bought a further, neighbouring sub-division, Lot 49 (1880) and later (1886) a half of the original Lot 50. The total area thus available for development totalled 82-ft frontage to Good

Hope Street. Prior to the partnership, in 1878, White had set up his timber workshop on his own land and carried on a prosperous business as principal timber supplier to the area. By 1881, and after the entry of Coghill, the workshop had given way to a dwelling house in which White himself lived. The remainder of Lot 48 together with the whole of Lot 49, plus the newly acquired slice of Lot 50, were now built upon by the timber merchant-entrepreneur and his less obvious partner. Five terrace houses within 5 years had thus been constructed, four of which were built specifically to let.

Armitage and Harris were another well-known pair of building developers in the Paddington area. Stephen W. Harris was a carpenter[16] but it is not clear what role was played by Armitage in the partnership. Harris was to live on the estate for some 6 years, in one of his own houses, and Armitage, although never living on the actual estate, did reside nearby. The 66-ft frontage of Lots 55 and 56, acquired by the pair in 1878, subsequently became four neat, double-storied terrace houses, christened 'Anne Terrace'—three of which were tenanted for most of the period and one of which was lived in by Harris until 1887.

Walter Hedges and his son John were both builders.[17] In 1878 they had bought Lot 59. By 1881 they owned Lots 58, 59, and 60. Together they proceeded to build what was possibly the finest terrace in Good Hope Street, 'Hampstead Terrace'. Hedges the elder was to live in one of them for the rest of his life. His son John lived four doors away at least until 1888. The five houses (each with a 20-ft frontage) were built concurrently throughout 1881. Thereafter, the three remaining houses were continuously tenanted until the end of the period under review.

Stockham, Ward, Davidson, Freeman, White and Coghill, Armitage and Harris, and Hedges and Son were all builders. Furthermore, they were small-time builders—often, it would appear, building their houses 'in instalments' over time rather than all at once. It appears that it was necessary to complete one and to consolidate finance before proceeding to build the next.[18] In only two of the instances outlined above were the

[16] Although *Sands Sydney Directory 1886* gives him as a 'builder'.

[17] Although 'Hedges and Son' is not given in the *Assessment Books*, *Sands Sydney Directory 1885* gives 'Hedges and Son' as 'builder and son'.

[18] The records of the St Joseph's Investment and Benefit Building Society (now Lisgar Investment and Building Society) reveal that numbers of small-scale builders in Paddington were able to finance a continuing operation via resort to building society funds. Between 1877 and 1890, 117 loans were granted to Paddington applications. Of the total of 65 borrowers for whom occupations are given in the records 19 were builders. Of these 6 were, between them, issued with 577 shares in the Society, i.e. £57,700. I am grateful to the Lisgar Investment and Building Society for making these records available to me.

small groups of terrace houses built contemporaneously. Together they provided the estate with 39 per cent (26 houses) of its total complement of houses, and included not only the most humble but also the most elegant.

In order to indicate the importance of the large developer for the Good Hope Estate it is first necessary to refer to those who, although not professional builders, were also engaged in small-scale development.

Stephen Whelan bought Lot 78 in 1878 from the trustees of the estate. 'Whelan Terrace', a neat pair of terrace houses, was completed and let within the year. Hancock (about whom little information is available) was an original purchaser of Lots 41 and 42. In 1876 he erected 'Harbour View House' upon portion of 41, which was to become his home from 1883 on. He subsequently sold all of Lot 42 and the remaining half of Lot 41. Cabinet-maker Abel Byarkman, the purchaser of Lot 46 in 1878 and of Lot 47 in 1879, built himself a house upon his initial purchase in 1878, sold portion of his second allotment in 1880, built a second house on the remaining portion of his first lot in 1887 (presumably using the funds acquired from re-sale), moved into it and rented out his first-built house. W. H. Lumsdaine, the boarding house proprietor noted earlier, after an amount of selling and re-selling of land, finally had two terrace houses built on his Lot 51, the first in 1884 and the second 4 years later. Nearby, on Lot 53, an expatriate Swiss warehouseman, J. M. Hungerbuhler, built his nostalgic 'St Gotthard' in 1879 (and sold it the following year); Peter Kling, a stonemason, built himself 'Eva Cottage' in 1880 on part of his purchase of Lot 37, as well as a house for rental in 1889; James Green in 1883 (Lot 40) and Patrick O'Carroll, a builder, in 1879 (Lot 43) each built themselves a house, as did the dairyman B. Laverty (Lot 45, 1880). M. F. O'Grady built 'Milton House' for his own use in 1880 (upon the portion of Lot 47 sold him by Abel Byarkman) and Peter Wahlberg, a builder, built himself 'Alster House' (or 'Alston House') in 1878 (Lot 54). In 1881 R. G. Peisley had erected a dwelling house on portion of Lot 41 and D. Sheehy, a contractor, whilst a tenant in 'Whelan Terrace' in 1885 and 1886, was having built his splendid free-standing, three-storied 'Avoca' with carriage way and stables (Lot 32, purchased 1884).

In all 20 houses were added to the estate by individual or non-professional builders. Few were speculators and fewer still were developers in the profit-making sense of the word. Added together, the small-time builder and the individual house builder provided the Good Hope Estate with 69 per cent of its total complement of houses.

The remaining 21 houses were built by two developers. The highest price at original sub-division, £6.10*s* per ft, had been paid by W. J.

McCarthy for land both adjoining his property Deepdene and fronting McCarthy's subsequent Deepdene Estate sub-division in 1880. The same two lots became eight (this time with frontages to Good Hope Street) and were sold to P. Moore. Within a year 'Moorefield Terrace' of seven two-storey houses had been built. Each was fully tenanted with an estimated annual rental value of £46 in 1882 rising to £65 a year later. One of Moore's lots remained as vacant land throughout the period. Although only an area of 20 ft by 95 ft this land, because of its commercial value, was given an estimated capital value of £320 in 1882 rising to £360 the following year. Since a considerable capital expenditure had been involved both in land purchase (foot/frontage prices averaging £8.2*s*) and in construction cost and since all houses were built at the same time, Moore, initially a coachbuilder but now landlord for a further eight houses in Paddington, can be classified as a large developer, engaged in rental investment.

The other large developer of the Good Hope Estate was Dr Edwin Horace T. Bottrell. By 1893 Bottrell owned 39 houses either on or within the immediate locality of the Good Hope Estate.[19] His purchase in 1886 of the only remaining section of land of any consequence on the estate, Lots 22 to 27, from widow Ridley[20] allowed, after demolition of the Ridley house, a terrace of thirteen houses to be built by 1891.[21]

These two men were absentee landlords in the sense of the word normally associated with terrace house development in nineteenth-century Sydney. They were also the only ones who could be categorized as such. Both owned rented property elsewhere in Paddington, and both built their housing developments as a whole development rather than over time as had been the case with the smaller developer. Moreover their respective developments account for the two largest rows of terrace houses on the estate. Even here, however, the essential local character of the development process was not disturbed. Moore, at about the same time as his Good Hope Estate venture, also purchased the grand mansion 'Ormond Hall' some 150 yards distant from the Good Hope Estate whilst Dr Bottrell lived in relative splendour in nearby Olive Bank Villa. Indeed, Bottrell was surrounded on three sides

19 Thirteen were in Glenmore Road (a hundred yards distant from the Good Hope Estate) each rented at £1.4*s* per annum; eight were further along the same road rented at £1.8*s*; five were in nearby Cooper Street rented at £1.2*s*, as well as the thirteen discussed here, each let at £1.4*s* per week.

20 The Presbyterian Rev. Ridley had consolidated his Good Hope Street holding from an initial 132-ft frontage in 1877 to a final 198 ft by 1881.

21 Each house was given an annual rental value of £30 in 1892. By 1890, however, rental values show a significant downturn (presumably on account of depressed economic conditions) and are thus misleading in the context outlined above.

by his housing speculations. Less than 50 yards to the west stood his thirteen Good Hope Street terraced houses. During the 1890s he built further houses both to the north and to the south of his imposing personal residence. But these large developers were exceptional on the estate. Between them they accounted for no more than 30 per cent of houses built.

That the majority of houses built, at least after 1883 when the building boom was at its height, were built for eventual tenancy seems beyond doubt. This activity does, however, mask the actual process of development whereby the small developer (often an owner-occupier—even if he did later become landlord of his originally self-occupied house) accounted for some 69 per cent of total houses built. Thus whilst it seems true that the Good Hope Estate was 'built to let' it is not sufficient to claim that the role of owner-occupier was insignificant. It is unlikely that the estate would have been developed as early (the absence of the large developers being remarkable in the years of most rapid growth) or indeed, as individually, had not the developer of limited means been the first to undertake the task. Further, the men who speculated in land and the men who built houses either for owner-occupancy or for rental were locals. There is little evidence to suggest that the whole character of development was other than 'domestic'. Even if developers did not live, at least for some time, on the estate they almost always lived within the municipality. It was the local small man rather than the outsider who undertook the development as well as the risk. The notion that Sydney's nineteenth-century suburbs were the result of large-scale impersonal development is shown to be a myth if the Good Hope Estate is at all representative, but much more research will have to be undertaken before this can be determined with authority.

IV

The Good Hope sub-division was only one of nine such sub-divisions in Paddington between 1875 and 1885, five of which were substantial. An analysis similar to that outlined above has been applied to the three largest—the Underwood (or Paddington) Estate (1876), the Olive Bank Estate (1878), and the Duxford Estate (1885). Between them they accounted for roughly 100 acres—a quarter of Paddington's total area. They initially brought onto the market a total of 835 allotments (606, 89 and 140 respectively). As the result of this analysis a number of general conclusions emerge.

The general pattern established by the Good Hope Estate can be regarded as typical for the municipality.

The sub-dividing and building of Paddington was not the result of large-scale development by absentee speculators.

The period of most active sub-division 1875 to 1885 marked the most rapid rates of increase in prices paid for land. Before the mid-1870s price rises had been slight. In 10 years and five major sub-divisions later land prices had at least doubled. In the process the few large landowners were replaced by a large number of medium-size landowners. More pertinent is that of the owners of newly sub-divided land a high proportion were builders. Thus it was frequently the builder himself who owned the land upon which he built.

The majority of Paddington houses were built for letting. This fact does, however, obscure the actual process of building activity. Because those who built were essentially small builders there was an element of 'transitional owner-occupation' whereby a builder, having completed one house of a terrace would live in it until able to re-finance and so continue with the building of his second or third house. The evidence is sufficiently strong to suggest that this procedure was common practice.

The predominance of the small-scale operator does much to explain the particular characteristic of overall Paddington development. It is rare to find a terrace exceeding six or seven houses. Even then the row could have taken 5 or 6 years to build. The striking fact is that by the mid-1880s over 60 per cent of rental houses were owned by landlords whose property holding did not exceed four houses, and about one-third of these were owned by landlords renting only one or two houses. Again, even the landlord owning from five to ten houses rarely had them in one line—normally his houses were scattered, in small groups of two, three and four, throughout the suburb. Terraces exceeding (say) eight houses were mainly built towards the end of the period and after the building boom had reached its peak; only then did the large developer play a significant role in the creation of the suburb. By this time, however, the principal characteristics of Paddington had been determined—by the small man.

In almost every instance, whether in land speculation, builder-development or non-builder development, the individual involved was a Paddington resident. The domestic nature of Paddington growth helps to explain the degree of municipal pride overt at the century's close. The small-scale landlord (holding more than 60 per cent of tenanted houses by 1885 at a time when only 26 per cent of total houses were owner-occupied) was a Paddington man. At the same date one-fifth of tenanted dwellings had the landlord living next door.

University of New South Wales

GRAEME DAVISON

PUBLIC UTILITIES AND THE EXPANSION OF MELBOURNE IN THE 1880s

The history of Australian cities is peculiarly the history of suburbs. The suburbs are where most Australians have lived; a large share of our resources have been absorbed in building and maintaining them. One part of that vast enterprise has been mainly a private activity; we like to build and buy our own homes. The other part has been largely public: city-dwellers, as much as isolated farmers, have looked to central public authorities to provide supporting services. This article describes the construction of public utilities in Melbourne during its most spectacular phase of growth—the land and building boom of the 1880s. These developments, of course, are best understood against the social and demographic patterns which they shaped and served.

In the period from 1881 to 1891, the population of 'greater Melbourne' increased from 284,874 to 491,700. Of this increase (206,926) only about 30 per cent was absorbed by the 7 municipalities[1] which, in 1881, had domiciled about 70 per cent of the city's population. Certainly great new tracts of these 'old' municipalities were opened up in this period: Abbotsford and Clifton Hill in Collingwood, Albert Park and Middle Park in South Melbourne, parts of North Fitzroy, North Carlton in the City of Melbourne, North Richmond and Burnley in Richmond, Balaclava and Elwood in St Kilda, Windsor and Armadale in Prahran. Nevertheless the main share of the population increase was claimed by other, 'newer' municipalities on their borders. Some of the largest population increases (in percentage terms) were in the hitherto relatively undeveloped northern and western suburbs (Essendon, Flemington and Kensington, Brunswick, Footscray) whose lack of scenic attractions were perhaps compensated by proximity to the central city.[2]

Population statistics, however, are but a guide to the physical process of suburban expansion. In Melbourne, perhaps more than in any

[1] The City of Melbourne itself, South Melbourne, Richmond, Collingwood, Fitzroy, Hotham (North Melbourne), St Kilda.

[2] The development of Brunswick, Northcote, Footscray and Kensington, however, cannot be understood apart from the growth of their 'staple' industries (brickworks, metals and engineering, saleyards and abattoirs). The dimensions of growth are summarized in Table 4 of Professor McCarty's essay.

other city in the world,[3] large and rapid population growth was handled without a dramatic alteration in population densities. In almost all suburbs the single family detached or semi-detached house remained the basic residential unit; most houses were of only one storey and had an attached garden. The obvious result of such largess of private space was a suburban sprawl unrivalled anywhere but on the west coast of the United States. This pattern of growth, moreover, demanded the provision–largely through government agencies–of a vast network of transport, communications and essential services. To assert that this style of suburban development was wasteful would perhaps prejudge the values which it expressed or too readily endorse those of European urbanism; nevertheless it was certainly expensive.

From an international standpoint, Melbourne's suburbs were also remarkable for their social homogeneity. In class terms, the segregation of suburbs seemed less marked than in European cities. E. E. Morris was impressed by Melbourne's 'diversity':[4] 'a poor house stands side by side with a good house; a cottage, one might almost say a hovel, in close proximity to a palace'. The pressures which set physical as well as social distance between classes were perhaps less imperative than those which operated in English cities. There, it has been argued, the middle class suburb was 'both an invention for accentuating . . . social distinctions and a means to putting off for a generation or two the full realization of what was entailed in living in a slum'.[5] Melbourne's few slums were 'easily rectifiable' in comparison with the 'gigantic evils of overcrowding and impecuniosity in London and other large English towns';[6] the intrusion of the lower orders upon middle class awareness was sometimes irritating and embarrassing,[7] but rarely traumatic or dangerous as it was in England. In such relatively frictionless conditions the pressures for the social differentiation of suburbs were mainly generated by economy or a mutual interest of *all* classes in the limitation of invidious comparison:

> All the world over, whether in the seven-flat tenements of Edinburgh or the purlieus of Paris, in London's conservative West End, or New York's equally exclusive Fifth Avenue, the rich live with the rich, and

[3] The *Victorian Yearbook 1888-9*, p. 488, recorded that population densities in Melbourne were lower than almost any other sizable city outside Australia. Also see Adna F. Weber, *The Growth of Cities in the Nineteenth Century*, New York 1899, p. 139.

[4] In E. E. Morris (ed.), *Picturesque Australasia*, Vol. I, p. 58.

[5] H. J. Dyos, 'The Slums of Victorian London', *Victorian Studies*, Vol. XI, No. 1 (September 1967), p. 27; and see his *Victorian Suburb*, Leicester 1961, Chapter 1.

[6] 'Australian Opinion and English Social Ills' in *Age*, 2 February 1884, p. 13.

[7] 'Our Street' by a Resident in *Australasian*, 26 February 1881 and 12 August 1881.

the poor with the poor. The palace and the hovel, except in the imagination of the socialistic romancer, seldom adjut. Contiguity and its inseparable contrast have never yet served to increase the happiness of either class. In prosperous Victoria, this contrast, when apparent, is chiefly one of comfort *versus* luxury, extreme poverty being rarely a constituent. The cottage may sometimes be overshadowed by the mansion but it is usually a very respectable cottage which has no occasion to be ashamed of itself. It is doubtful, however, whether its inmates would not be happier if in less close proximity to their richer brethren whose wealthier lot is calculated to excite envy and discontent in the average bosom. The fact of an Englishman's house being his castle does not render him oblivious to its insignificance when compared with the palatial dimensions of his neighbour's stronghold. He is fully alive to the disproportionate, and utterly abhors being, in any sense, looked down upon. Hence it is, partly, that, in Melbourne, such class distinctions meet with the observance accorded them elsewhere, an obedience to the social law which takes its root from this perception of the fitness of things.[8]

The social differentiation of suburbs may be charted in two ways. One proceeds through contemporaries' evaluations of the status of particular suburbs[9]—for example the 'guide-book' descriptions which rated Toorak as an 'upper class' suburb, Hawthorn as a 'superior middle class suburb', Collingwood as a 'poorer class' suburb.[10] But such tags are notoriously euphemistic, and constitute, at best, a first approach to the problem. The second method relies on 'objective' data; it plots the geographical distribution of population or residence characteristics selected as indices of 'social rank'.[11] The data most suitable to this purpose—occupational returns of suburban areas—was not published in this period.[12] Nevertheless statistics of the size of dwellings may furnish a reliable, if fairly crude, substitute. It has to be assumed that a suburb with a high proportion of houses with more than six rooms is likely to be a prestigious suburb and that one with a low proportion of large

[8] *Australasian Building Societies' and Mortgage Companies' Gazette*, hereafter *ABSG*.

[9] For a modern study using this general approach see Athol Congalton, *Status Ranking of Sydney Suburbs*, Sydney 1961.

[10] *Argus*, 6 September 1884, p. 13; 29 November 1884, p. 4, and 9 August 1884, p. 13.

[11] For a modern Australian study in this tradition see F. L. Jones, 'A Social Ranking of Melbourne Suburbs', *Australian and New Zealand Journal of Sociology*, Vol. 3, No. 2 (October 1967), pp. 93-110.

[12] R. J. Johnston, 'The Location of high status residential areas', *Geografiska Annaler*, 48, Ser. B (1966), pp. 23-35, attempts a definition of Melbourne's high status areas in 1861 and 1888, the latter through locating 'high class' individuals' residences on an urban plan.

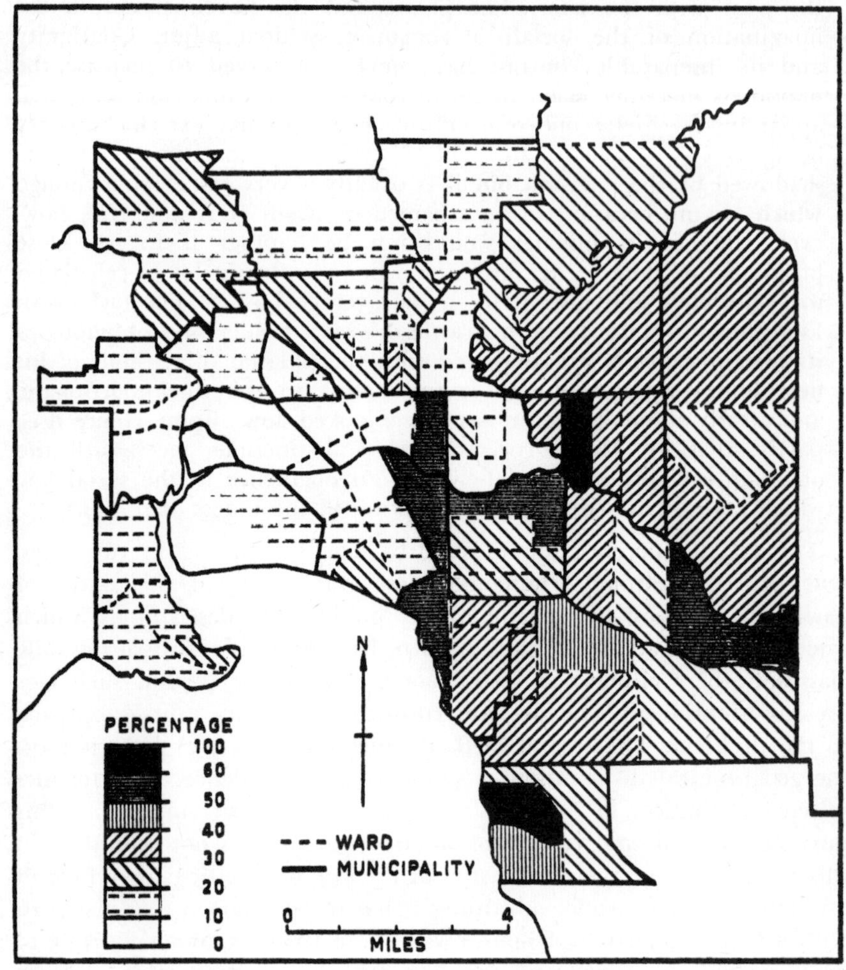

Map 1—Percentages of Houses of more than Six Rooms by Wards or Municipalities, 1891

houses is likely to be an invidious suburb.[13]

The distribution of large houses at the Census of 1891 is shown in Map 1. According to this evidence, the most significant concentrations of high status areas were on the high south and east banks of the Yarra above Prince's Bridge, by the sea at St Kilda and Brighton, and through the undulating, sand-soil areas to the east of the Yarra. Low

[13] This assumption can be partially substantiated. An examination of municipal ratebooks suggests that the size of houses related more closely to occupational status (and servant requirements) than to family size.

status areas, on the other hand, were grouped on the river flats of the Yarra and Saltwater (Maribyrnong) Rivers and on the flat, basalt plains to the north and west of the city.

The association of elevated areas with high social status was supported by medical, aesthetic and symbolic considerations. A house on a hill or by the seaside was considered healthier than others. According to theories that were still current in Victoria, disease was spread through noxious 'vapours' and was, correctly, associated with the disposal of human and other wastes. Hill and seaside sites were exposed to breezes and fresh air, remote from foetid swamps and rivers and favoured with natural drainage. Real estate agents interpreted suburban mortality statistics with an innocent disregard for nutrition, medical services, hygiene, education, and the age structures of the population and with a ritual acknowledgement of the efficacy of 'fresh air'. That Footscray was foul and Hawthorn healthy was perhaps as much a result, as it was a proof, of the popular theory of disease. Hill sites were favoured, secondly, because they were supposed to give access to 'a view'. There is no feature of real estate advertisements of this period more surprising than the number of sites, now quite enclosed by terra cotta and flapping bed linen, which were said to command panoramic views of all Melbourne, its suburbs, the Bay and surrounding countryside. Finally, living on a hill symbolized the householder's position in the social pyramid.[14] In this connection, the direct confrontation of the most prestigious suburbs (Toorak, South Yarra, Kew) and the least prestigious (Collingwood, Burnley, South Richmond) across the river suggests there is something in the view that suburban differentiation had the effect, at least at the extremes, of actually '*accentuating* social distinctions'.

The providers of public utilities in the 1880s had to operate within the framework set by these broad patterns of population growth, density and social differentiation. And in turn, of course, the developing network of public utilities was itself to exert a powerful influence upon the pace and shape of suburban growth. Transport is perhaps the clearest illustration of their reciprocal influence. Contemporary railways officials actually began with an unrealistic view of the primacy of transport in suburban development. For example, William Fitzpatrick, a deputy traffic manager of the Victorian Railways, asserted that

> very early in the history of this city a railway system was established which induced people to go and live outside it, so much that our vast suburban system has been created in that way. I doubt if you

[14] For discussion of these matters see *ABSG*, 13 June 1886, pp. 117-18.

> will find a city of the same importance where so few of the inhabitants live in the city itself.[15]

Supporters of this view believed that 'the proper principle to adopt was to make railways precede population and not population railways',[16] and held that

> within a radius of a few miles of Melbourne . . . , there can be no mistake made with regard to the construction of those railways. The tendency of Melbourne is to reside outside the city, and the greater the opportunity you afford for getting to and fro the more rapid will be the development and the expansion of the suburbs.[17]

New railway extensions were not designed to supply estimated social requirements; indeed railways' ministers and commissioners expressed a general scepticism about such estimates. Introducing the 1884 'Octopus' Bill, Duncan Gillies avowed that

> on one point I will follow the example of a predecessor [Bent]. I will not submit to the House estimates of the probable receipts from the proposed lines. Years ago I arrived at the conclusion that these estimates were wholly unreliable.[18]

Since estimates were unreliable, the question of probable demand was set aside. The railways would simply create their own demand.

These were simple assumptions indeed, for the part which railways played in suburban growth has to be understood in relation to both their technical characteristics (compared with trams, omnibuses, etc.) and to the social needs and position of their prospective clienteles. While trains travelled faster (20 m.p.h.) than trams (8 to 10 m.p.h.), trams ran more frequently and, in general, picked up passengers nearer to their homes and dropped them closer to their destinations. With the traveller from suburb to the city centre, it followed, *ceteris paribus*, that the further he resided from the centre of the city, the more likely he was to travel by train rather than tram.[19]

[15] Evidence to the Board appointed to enquire into the Working and Management of the Railways, *VPP* 71/1895-6, Q. 1911. For similar statements see *Argus*, 1 January 1889, p. 7F.

[16] David Gaunson quoted *Argus*, 15 October 1884, remarks on the 'Octopus' Bill.

[17] Richard Speight (Chief Commissioner) in evidence to the Parliamentary Standing Committee on Railways 1891, Enquiry into the Northern Lines, *VPP* 3/1891 Q. 2.

[18] Quoted *Argus*, 8 October 1884, p. 6. For similar assertions see evidence of Speight, loc. cit., Q. 57.

[19] On the technology of trams see article of W. C. Kernot in Alexander Sutherland (ed.), *Victoria and its Metropolis*, Vol. II, Melbourne 1888, pp. 17-23, and his *The Extension of Rail and Tramways*, Melbourne 1887. The consequences of these differences are discussed in the evidence to the Parliamentary Standing Committee on Railways 1891, Enquiry into the Northern Lines, loc. cit.; see especially evidence of Speight (Qs. 1, 133, 151, 189) and to the Board on the Working and Management of the Railways, loc. cit., especially evidence of Robert Lockhead (Qs. 1362-5).

Secondly, since the initial and recurrent costs[20] of railway operation were generally higher than the costs of trams, a system of fares geared directly to costs tended to draw the rich to trains, and the poor to trams. In fact, railway costs were spread among passengers by a system of varying fares: first and second class, weekly, monthly, and yearly tickets.

The most notable extension of railway travel to the poor came through the provision of special 'workmen's tickets'. In January 1882, a number of workingmen from Footscray and Williamstown petitioned the Minister of Railways for special workingmen's trains to be run at reduced fares.[21] Within two weeks Bent had acceded to the request and workingmen's trains began running on all the main suburban lines—two in the morning and two in the evening—at the special rate of 2d for all journeys under 5 miles and 3d for all over 5 miles.[22] The new service proved popular: ticket sales rose from 1,600 in late February to 2,200 in March. The minister was justified in expanding the service, especially with early morning trains.[23] Separate returns of traffic on workingmen's trains were not published, but to judge from the number of scheduled services, they appear to have expanded even further during the rest of the decade. In 1883 there were 32 workingmen's services daily; in 1887 there were 59.[24] Nevertheless despite—and perhaps even because of—such innovations, social distinctions persisted between train and tram travel and since it was broadly true that lower class individuals resided in inner areas and upper class in outer areas, these tended to reinforce the technical adaptation of trains to outer and trams to inner areas. These relationships are confirmed by the statistics of railway traffic (Table 1) which suggest that outer areas, especially in the south and east, had high rates of use while inner and northern areas supplied relatively few passengers.

The story of the part played by rail and tramways in suburban development is of the gradual and mutually destructive interpenetration of each system upon the other's catchment areas. The Melbourne railways system in 1880 was a recently contracted (but unconsummated)[25] union of the privately owned Hobson's Bay Railway Company which had operated most of the lines to the south and east of the city, and

20 Kernot, loc. cit., points out that the basic costs of cable tram operation did not vary with the number of cars which operated on a given line; energy input was constant.

21 *Argus*, 14 January 1882 and 13 April 1882.

22 Ibid., 25 January 1882. As a further concession, tickets could be purchased in bundles of 1/9 or 2/6 for 12.

23 *Age*, 9 March 1882, p. 3; *Argus*, 28 February, 6 March 1882.

24 *Book Timetables of the Victorian Railways*, 1883, 1884-5, 1887.

25 The two termini were actually connected in 1879; but effective knitting together of the two networks had to wait for the Flinders Street Viaduct which was not opened until 1891.

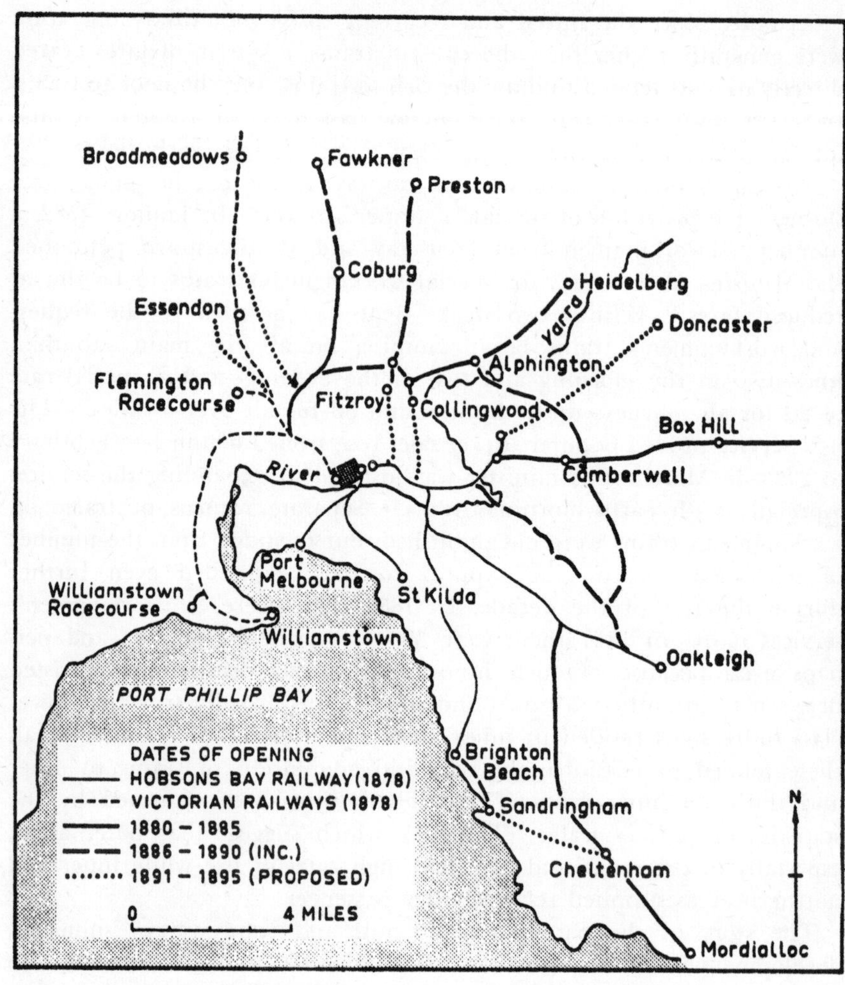

Map 2—MELBOURNE RAILWAY SYSTEM, 1880 TO 1895

the Victorian (Government's) Railways which owned the lines to the north and west of the city (see Map 2). In 1880 the Berry Government enacted a bill (Act 44 Victoria 862) to extend the suburban system with new lines to Coburg in the north, Camberwell and Lilydale in the east, Mordialloc in the south, from Richmond to Alphington through the densely populated Collingwood district and from Alphington to Prince's Hill. The cost of resuming valuable urban land and the opposition of local residents to level crossings forced the government to abandon the Richmond-Alphington line.[26] But the line from Prince's Hill was built

[26] *Argus*, 18 November 1880, 13 April, 15 September, and 1, 5, 13, 28 October 1881, and 8, 29 March, and 25 August 1882.

Table 1

OUTWARD TRAIN JOURNEYS PER UNIT OF SUBURBAN POPULATION

Suburb	1881	1891
Essendon	93	147
Flemington and Kensington	130	156
Brunswick	—	17
Hawthorn	183	182
Footscray	132	148
Kew	—	9
Brighton	178	171
Prahran	127	154
St Kilda	130	77
Richmond	75	127
South Melbourne	46	98
Port Melbourne	72	128
Collingwood	—	11
Fitzroy	—	5
Hotham	10	61

Source: Victorian Railways Report of the Board of Land and Works *VPP* 48/1882-3, Appendix 16; Report of the Victorian Railways Commissions *VPP* 124/1891, Appendix 17; and *Victorian Census* 1881 and 1891. These calculations are fairly crude since traffic through particular stations had to be assigned to the population of a municipality which may not have corresponded to the 'catchment area' of the station.

and, though separated from the main suburban network, operated for a time with carriages driven by a gas engine.[27]

During the debates on the 1880 Act, ministers and members of Parliament were besieged by deputations of local worthies urging the fullest development of railways in their districts and often pressing for proposed railways to be re-routed to conform with the general, or some more personal, interest.[28] Rarely did they show, or even seem obliged to show, that the proposed new lines would be economic. Sometimes new lines were urged on the ground that they would appreciate the value of government lands.[29] Usually they were regarded as a public service to which all districts were entitled as a matter of course. It was for this reason that the suburbs to the north of the city were especially aggrieved. There was strong support for the contention

[27] *Victorian Engineer*, 15 June 1886, p. 519.

[28] Allegations of 'jobbing' were frequent; it was commonly said, for example, that Bent had seen Brighton unusually well served for railway services and that O'Shanassy had secured the re-routing of the Camberwell line through his own property. But such accusations are difficult to substantiate. See for example Geoffrey Blainey, *A History of Camberwell*, Melbourne 1964, pp. 49-50.

[29] In two cases where this argument was applied—the proposed railways to the Yarra Mouth and from St Kilda to Elwood—the government was evidently not persuaded. See *Argus*, 10, 11 August 1882, and 16, 31 October 1884.

that 'the northern districts, which [had] been neglected for so long should have a fair share of the plunder that was going on'.[30]

In 1882 Thomas Bent proposed a second instalment of railway extension which was actually to make notable concessions to the northern districts. His bill included a line from Royal Park to Prince's Hill, with a 'cockspur' to Fitzroy, an extension to Northcote, and some elements of the controversial 'outer circle' line. The 'outer circle' was already a project with a considerable history: it had been first proposed in the early 'seventies by Thomas Higinbotham, then Manager of the Victorian Railways, as a means of bringing the Gippsland line to a city terminal. This he hoped to achieve by constructing a great 'outer circle' of railway from Oakleigh through Camberwell, Alphington, Clifton Hill, and North Melbourne to the Spencer Street terminal. In addition, it was supposed that the new line would 'open up' a tract of hitherto undeveloped, but promising, suburbs.[31]

Bent's bill perished with the O'Loghlen Government in 1883. Yet, in spite of the opprobrium[32] surrounding his administration (which led to the transfer of some ministerial powers to a Board of Railways Commissioners) his successor, Duncan Gillies, in 1884 produced an even more extravagant bill.[33] It included extensions of existing lines from Coburg to Somerton,[34] from Royal Park to Prince's Hill, from Prince's Hill to Fitzroy and Collingwood together with a new line from Burnley to Oakleigh through Glen Iris[35] and the whole of the ardently canvassed 'outer circle' connection.[36] In addition the Parliament passed, as an amendment, a line from Hawthorn to Kew which had been

[30] Reid quoted ibid., 30 April 1884, p. 9. For reports of the earlier agitation see ibid., 16, 17 September 1880, and 5, 20 July 1883.

[31] Leo Harrigan, *Victorian Railways to '62*, Melbourne 1962, pp. 101-8. As critics pointed out at the time, these were most dubious grounds for such an expensive policy: there was no longer any need for the Gippsland railway to terminate at Spencer Street which, in any case, would be shortly joined to the Flinders Street terminal; it was very doubtful whether householders could be induced to live on the 'outer circle' by which route the journey to work would be longer and more expensive than by any of the old 'Hobson's Bay' lines. See 'Engineer' in *Argus*, 21 October 1884.

[32] Especially because of the notorious 'Kensington Hill Job'. See M. Cannon, *The Landboomers*, Melbourne 1966, pp. 39-40.

[33] Bent's bill proposed a total of 915 miles of suburban and country railway; Gillies' bill proposed 927 miles.

[34] Note agitation for this *Argus*, 15 August 1883.

[35] Deputations ibid., 5 July, 11 August 1882. There were allegations that the line was a 'job'. Ibid., 17 October 1884.

[36] Apart from the obvious beneficiaries in the Balwyn-Canterbury area (see meeting ibid., 22 October 1884), perhaps the most ardent support of the 'outer circle' came from brick company interests in Brunswick looking for a better supply of firewood from Gippsland (ibid., 2, 28 June, 2 August 1883).

included in Bent's bill but inexplicably omitted from Gillies'.[37] By making systematic mutual concessions to local interests (collusion?), the Parliament virtually abandoned economic calculation as a basis for suburban railways policy. Charles H. Pearson, himself a railway advocate, was among the few who spared some thought for the possible consequences of passing '900 miles of railway, involving an expenditure of four millions, without any information, without any discussion, and amid shouts of laughter'.[38] The 'Octopus' Bill, as it came to be called, was a striking illustration of the thesis that 'the usual parliamentary methods [were] quite unsuitable for a developmental policy'.[39]

The lines passed in 1884 were gradually completed during the second half of the 'eighties; few were in operation before 1888-90. By this time, however, further extensions were projected. Although they were never carried out, they deserve attention as the logical culmination of the policies initiated in 1880-4. The commissioners proposed[40] to build new lines from Newmarket to Keilor Road and from Royal Park to Pascoevale in the north,[41] from Kew to Doncaster and Doncaster to Bulleen Road in the east, from Sandringham to Cheltenham in the south. The most important and controversial extensions, however, were those from Prince's Bridge to Fitzroy and Collingwood. And for these, most arguments came down to a simple assertion that 'the south has railways and that the north ought to have them'.[42] If the financial depression had not curtailed investment, the railways commissioners might indeed have pursued, far into alien territory, the reckless policy of building railways in accordance with political pressures rather than economic demand.

In some respects the building of the tramways was a more rational

[37] The excuse for dropping the line was the heavy cost of earthworks but this certainly did not convince the deputations which protested against the new minister's action (ibid., 8 October 1884 (editorial), 11, 17 October 1884).

[38] Ibid., 22 October 1884, p. 7.

[39] F. W. Eggleston, *State Socialism in Victoria*, London 1932, p. 45.

[40] Statement . . . by the Victorian Railways Commissioners [on] Proposed new lines of Railway in *VPP* A1/1890.

[41] The first seems to have passed through part of Thomas Bent's 'Heights of Maribyrnong Estate' (see M. Cannon, op. cit., p. 182); the latter certainly did pass through lands owned by Bent, Munro, Melville, Woods and other parliamentarians on the eastern bank of the Moonee Ponds Creek (*Argus*, 19 July 1892). Hence 'Oriel's' little rhyme:

> It [Pascoevale line] ran past 'eligible lots' and 'splendid situations',
> And after well-known patriots they named the leading stations.
> You heard the porter ring his bell, and cry with special unction—
> Next train for Bent Town, Munroville, La Rose and Melville Junction.
>
> (*Argus*, 23 July 1892).

[42] Parliamentary Standing Committee on Railways Enquiry into the Northern Lines, *VPP* 3/1891, Qs. 465, 1295-6.

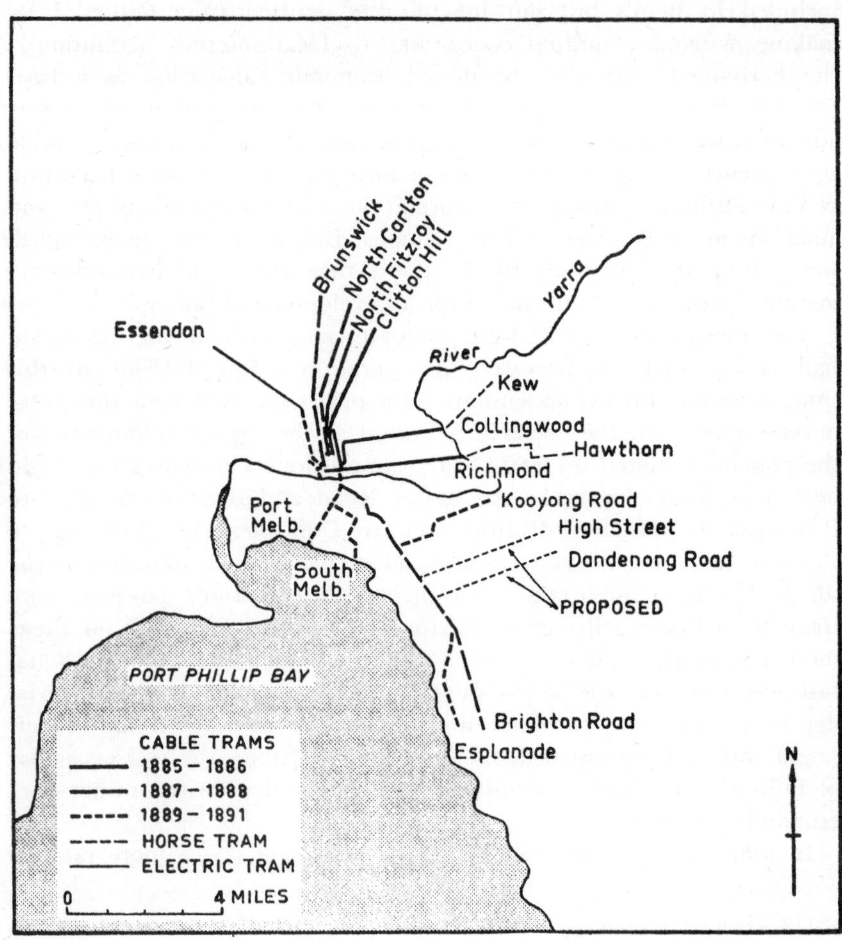

Map 3—Melbourne Tramway System, 1880 to 1895

operation. From the time of the foundation of his Melbourne Omnibus Company in the 1860s, F. B. Clapp had looked forward to the ultimate establishment of a tramway system. According to the company's Secretary (W. G. Sprigg), 'every property it bought, every building it put up was carefully planned with a view to the future [street] railway system'.[43] The tracks of the new tramway system were actually to follow the old omnibus routes almost exactly.[44] In 1881 Clapp's plans were

[43] Before an unnamed parliamentary committee quoted *Argus*, 9 November 1935 (in Kenyon Cuttings, Vol. I, p. 68 in State Library of Victoria).

[44] Compare Wimpole's *Guide to Melbourne*, 1881, pp. 86ff. and tram routes as given, for example, in Alexander Sutherland, op. cit., Vol. II, pp. 22-3.

upset by the appearance of Henry Hoyt who formed a Victorian tramway company with the intention of establishing lines through several of the inner suburban areas. However, despite the concurrence of some of the municipalities, there was widespread antagonism to Hoyt's scheme and a proposed bill was dropped. In 1883 the Service Government established a tramways trust with formal control over tramways in most central municipalities. Clapp bought out Hoyt's company and the Melbourne Tramway and Omnibus Company, having persuaded the Parliament of the superiority of cable trams over other types,[45] was granted a lease to operate in the 13 municipalities until the lines were handed back to the trust in 1916.

The company's first routes were confined to the inner suburbs: Richmond (1885), Fitzroy (1886), Collingwood and Clifton Hill (1887) along Nicholson Street (1887), Brunswick (1887) and Carlton (1887). Trams entered the 'city mile' by several routes and it was an intended result that the central business district was provided with a close network of tram transport.[46] In the later 'eighties, however, the tramways managers, victims of lowering interest rates and rising expectations, began to extend their operations further afield into 'railway territory': to St Kilda and Brighton roads (1888), Prahran (1889), North Melbourne, West Melbourne, Port Melbourne (1890) and St Kilda Esplanade (1891). Horse trams, more economical for light traffic, were introduced on the Kew and Hawthorn routes (see Map 3). There were schemes for additional lines in Prahran[47] and for a service from Collingwood to St Kilda designed mainly, it would seem, to transport artisans expeditiously to the seaside.[48] The inapplicability of the tramways to outer suburban transport is evident in the traffic figures given in Table 2.

The further the tramways extended into the outer suburbs, the poorer became their passenger/mile returns. Of course, the system as a whole may well have remained profitable; the returns upon the company's early years of operation had been prodigious. Nevertheless it was becoming evident that the penetration of trams into railway 'catchment areas', like the railways' invasion of tramways' territory to the north of

[45] See especially evidence to Select Committee . . . on Melbourne Tramways Bill. *VPP* 1884 *passim*. Sydney, of course, had adopted steam trams but her experience was not such as to encourage the 'sister' colony. See for example *Australian Engineering and Building News*, 1 May 1880, p. 240.

[46] See Select Committee . . . on Melbourne Tramways, loc. cit., Q. 100.

[47] Select Committee on Tramways Act 1890 Amendment Bill, *VPP* 1891. The new lines would add to the already existing lines along Toorak Road, parallel tracks along High Street and Dandenong Road to Kooyong Road.

[48] Report and evidence of Select Committee . . . on the Suburban Tramways Company Bill, *VPP* 1890, Qs. 5, 48.

Table 2

TRAMWAYS TRAFFIC AND RECEIPTS, 1886 TO 1891

Year	Miles open	Tram mileage (millions)	Passengers carried (millions)	Receipts £'000	Passengers per mile run	Receipts (shillings) per mile run
1886	2.3	0.5	16.4	189	32.9	7.6
1887	7.6	1.5	18.0	207	11.9	2.8
1888	19.9	4.0	31.1	363	7.7	1.8
1889	31.0	6.4	45.0	527	7.0	1.7
1890	37.2	7.5	45.3	527	6.1	1.4
1891	45.3	9.2	48.0	563	5.2	1.2

Source: *Victorian Yearbook*, 1892, p. 161.

the city, constituted a source of potential difficulty and conflict. From the passenger's viewpoint, however, the interpenetration of the two services produced a transport system of exceptional extent, cheapness, variety and efficiency.

Melbourne's transport system was perhaps the most serious and spectacular example of maladjustment in the relationship between the provision of public utilities and suburban growth. But there were others. The 'essential services'—water, sewerage, gas, roads—were, as their name implies, necessary but never really decisive in setting the pace and shape of development. They generally followed in the wake of the private developers and railway promoters, retarding their schemes only on the significantly few occasions when they failed to match the developers' pace.

The provision of roads and drains and such primitive sewerage as existed was a responsibility of local municipalities. However it was not until 1890 that councils were empowered, under the Health Act, to supervise and undertake street construction and to recover from the owners of adjoining properties the costs of all necessary works.[49] The published returns of local government finance are not sufficiently detailed to recover estimates of the amounts spent specifically on street construction; nevertheless some more detailed returns available for 1888 and 1889 suggest that 'new' suburbs like Hawthorn, Northcote, and Brunswick were spending a larger proportion of their total revenue for the purpose.[50] Although spiralling land values increased revenue from rates, local government bodies borrowed heavily during this period. Between 1883 and 1892 Victorian municipalities borrowed about

[49] Act 1098 (1890), Section 234.

[50] *Victorian Statistical Registers*, 'Population'.

£1,875,700 in London.[51] Much of this, however, was probably devoted to less 'essential' projects, such as the palatial town halls which were the most evident legacy of this hey-day of municipal spending.

The disposal of night soil was usually undertaken by contractors on behalf of city or shire councils which either levied a special rate or included the cost in a general rate. The contractors collected the soil in special metal night carts, calling once a week between 11 p.m. and 3 a.m., and deposited it either on market gardens or farms on the outskirts of the metropolis.[52] Since gardeners were prepared to pay for manure, municipalities such as Brighton, Footscray, Port Melbourne and Prahran which adjoined open country were generally able to provide night soil disposal services more cheaply than the inner suburbs.[53] Councils and their employees evinced little interest in the method of disposal; one inspector who took the trouble to investigate was appalled at the threat to public health posed by the conditions of its use on market gardens.[54] Storm water, urine, and household drainage were fed into open drains and eventually flowed into the Yarra, the Saltwater River or one of their sluggish tributaries. Sometimes its progress was impeded by unfavourable landfall, blocked drains or poorly designed streets. As population became more concentrated, rivers and creeks more polluted, the cartage of night soil more onerous and its disposal more difficult and unhygienic, the need for some comprehensive, modern system of sewerage became imperative.

The story of the creation of the Melbourne and Metropolitan Board of Works and the building of the Melbourne sewerage system lies outside the scope of this article. Nevertheless, in view of her advanced transport, gas and other services, Melbourne's tardiness in this matter, especially in comparison with her rival capitals Sydney and Adelaide, calls for explanation. Melbourne, firstly, was not favoured by topography: unlike Sydney, whose sewage was conveyed by gravitation to an outfall in the ocean off Bondi, Melbourne was spread over an area too wide and low for a gravitational system and was without a suitable ocean outfall close to the centre of the city.[55] Furthermore,

[51] *Victorian Yearbook*, 1893, Vol. I, p. 234.

[52] Appendix A of First Progress Report of Royal Commission on the Sanitary Condition of the Metropolis, *VPP* 27/1889 (especially Qs. XVIII and XX); also see evidence to the Commission of Eassie (Qs. 3390-3407), Fullerton (Q. 6114) and Robertson (Q. 5968-70).

[53] Ibid., Appendix A, Q. XXI.

[54] Evidence of Eassie, loc. cit.

[55] *Victorian Engineer*, 15 June 1888, p. 7, Royal Commission on Sanitary Condition of the Metropolis, I, loc. cit., p. xiv and *Water Supply and Sewerage Systems of the Melbourne and Metropolitan Board of Works* compiled by George A. Gibbs, Melbourne 1925, pp. 53-4.

control of sanitation in Melbourne was divided among a score of local municipalities which were slow to recognize the problem and reluctant to surrender their powers to a necessary central authority.[56] Finally the provision of sanitation, unlike some other public utilities, was unregulated by competition. It was not until 1885 that a municipal conference was held to discuss the matter. In 1887 a draft bill for a Metropolitan Board of Works was placed before the government which, in turn, established a Royal Commission to investigate the sanitary condition of the metropolis and invited the eminent English engineer, James Mansergh, to make a report. In 1890 the Board was duly constituted but it was not until 1897 that the new sewerage system was actually in operation.

Water supply had been vested in a central authority since the 1850s, when the Yan Yean system was inaugurated. Since that time there had been piecemeal additions to the reticulation system but no extension of the catchment area or of storage reservoirs. Indeed, for a time, the water supply system was unequal to the prodigious demands of expansion. The summers of 1887 and 1888 brought complaints from the enraged residents of South Melbourne, Port Melbourne and Williamstown, who were unable, for days on end, to get water from their taps.[57] The difficulty did not lie in the sources of supply, for the old catchment had recently been augmented by the waters of Wallaby Creek (1885) and Silver Creek (1886) which increased the daily flow by some 12 million gallons.[58] (The Maroondah Dam, on the Watts River near Healesville, was begun in 1886 but not completed until 1891.) The main impediment to an adequate water supply was rather the reticulation system itself.[59] Several remedies were canvassed: meters, the introduction of an intermittent supply, separate systems for high or remote areas, a general increase in the size of street mains and service reservoirs. The first was rejected on the ground that any reasonable charge for excess water would not deter summer irrigators; the second because it would threaten public health. The third was employed only in the modified form of service reservoirs designed to fill at night or over periods of low demand and discharge at times when demand exceeded the mains flow. Such reservoirs were built at Essendon (1880, 1883), Caulfield (1883) and Kew (1886). A further large reservoir supplied

[56] *Victorian Engineer*, 15 August 1886, p. 8, 15 May 1888, p. 8.

[57] *Argus*, 1 December 1888.

[58] Melbourne and Metropolitan Board of Works, *A Historical Survey of Melbourne's Water Supply*, Melbourne 1942, pp. 17-18 and *Water Supply and Sewerage Systems . . .*, pp. 17-19.

[59] Professor Kernot in *Victorian Engineer*, 15 February 1887, pp. 5, 8.

by a direct pipe line from Yan Yean was opened at Surrey Hills in 1891.[60]

The provision of new mains–the principal means to the alleviation of the water shortage–proceeded in various parts of the metropolis with unequal vigour. Between 1880 and 1888 most mains construction was designed to increase flows to the expanding eastern suburbs and to supplement the main flow from Preston to the central city. But little was done to improve the mains to South Melbourne, Port Melbourne, Footscray, Williamstown and Essendon. After the crises of 1887 and 1888, however, a second 15 in. branch was provided for Williamstown and Footscray and 18 in. and 24 in. branches were run from the new 30 in. main to Essendon and South Melbourne.[61] Thus, by 1890, an adequate supply to all suburbs was assured.

In 1880 gas supply of the Melbourne metropolitan area within 8 miles of its centre, with three exceptions, was in the hands of a single company–the Metropolitan Gas Company–which had been formed 2 years earlier by the amalgamation of the City of Melbourne Gas and Coke Company, the Collingwood, Fitzroy and District Gas and Coke Company, and the South Melbourne Gas Company.[62] The Act of 1878 sanctioning the union and granting the monopoly, had excluded Brighton, Footscray and Williamstown; the first was served by the Brighton Gas Company (1878) and the latter two by the Footscray Gas Company (1878). Until about 1880 gas was used almost exclusively for street and domestic lighting. In that year, however, the first gas stoves, priced at about £6, were sold in Melbourne and in 1887 gas water-heating appliances appeared on the market.[63] Gas engines were increasingly used in industrial plants. The proportion of new gas connections to stoves grew spectacularly during the decade: by 1885, 12,000 had been installed and about 40 per cent of new connections in 1887 were for this purpose. By 1889 the proportion had risen to 60 per cent.[64] A large proportion of gas stoves were hired rather than pur-

60 *Water Supply and Sewerage Systems* . . . , p. 20. This was necessary because the elevation of some of the newer eastern suburbs was greater than that of the main supply reservoir at Preston.

61 Royal Commission on the Sanitary Condition of Melbourne, Second Progress Report, Water Supply of the Metropolitan Area, *VPP* 103/1889, p. 9, *Argus*, 6 December 1888, *Water Supply and Sewerage Systems* . . . , p. 36.

62 41 Victoria no. 586; see Metropolitan Gas Company, *Jubilee 1878-1928*, and Report of Select Committee of Legislative Assembly upon the Metropolitan Gas Company's Bill, *VPP* D(24)/1877-8.

63 C. H. Eddey, 'Appliance Sales' in *Compendium of Lectures delivered to Officers of the Metropolitan Gas Company*, Melbourne 1941, pp. 47-8. (The records of the Metropolitan Gas Company appear to have been destroyed.)

64 *Argus*, 28 May 1885, p. 6E; *Australasian Insurance and Banking Record*, henceforth AIBR, 16 August 1887, p. 482. See also Brighton Gas Company Director's Report, 16 July 1887 (in Defunct Companies no. 397) and Footscray Gas Com-

chased; in 1890 the Metropolitan Gas Company had 12,697 on hire.[65]

Such an active leasing policy suggests what other evidence confirms—that the gas companies were not content simply to cater to established demand, but were actively promoting gas consumption. Wherever their services fell short, there were competitors eager to annex their territory. In 1885, for example, when there were complaints of inadequate gas supply in the Prahran district, a rival company was formed in the hope of securing similar rights to the Metropolitan, only to be forestalled when the existing service was improved.[66] Similarly, the Brighton Gas Company was forced to press ahead and service new areas by the active competition of Thomas Bent's Central Brighton and Moorabbin Gas Company. The threatened entry of the new company was averted by its amalgamation with the old Brighton Company in 1887.[67]

Throughout the 'eighties, and especially after 1885, the Metropolitan Company attempted to lay its pipes and maintain supply well ahead of demand. In 1886 the Chairman (John Benn) reported that 'new and enlarged mains have been laid wherever there was a prospect of a payable return, so that there is scarcely any settled population within the company's area that is not supplied'.[68] And in 1887: 'Keeping ahead of demand was the only safe means of conveying to their consumers a constant and ample supply.'[69] The company had taken over 300 miles of mains in 1878; in 1890 there were 723 miles. In 1878 there were about 35,000 meter installations; in 1890 about 78,000.[70] On the production side, the company installed a new mechanically operated coaling plant, new retort stoking machinery and a large purifying and washing plant.[71] During the early 'eighties it erected new ½ million cu. ft capacity gas holders at Richmond and Fitzroy. When a further holder of 3 million cu. ft (more than double the required capacity) was undertaken in 1888, the Chairman explained to shareholders that

> the reasons are that the cost per 1000 feet holding capacity is much cheaper proportionally than the cost of a small one, and that with ample storage gas can be made at a cheaper rate, and with less

pany Directors' Report, February 1888 (Defunct Companies no. 416), *AIBR*, 16 August 1889, p. 576.

65 C. H. Eddey, loc. cit., p. 48.

66 *Argus*, 28 May 1885, p. 6E; *AIBR*, 14 August 1885, pp. 453-4. The South Suburban Gas Company formed in 1885 was voluntarily wound up in 1886.

67 Weston Bate, *A History of Brighton*, Melbourne 1962, pp. 208-11.

68 *AIBR*, 15 February 1886, pp. 76-7.

69 Ibid., 16 August 1887, p. 482.

70 Ibid., 16 August 1890, p. 576, 16 February 1888, p. 87.

71 H. E. Grove in *Compendium of Lectures*, pp. 17-18.

> strain on the manufacturing plant; also that it occupies about two years to complete a large holder from the time the work is commenced, and we must not disregard the fact that consumption has about doubled in the last five years.[72]

So confirmed was the company in its 'forward' policy that two further holders, each of 3 million cu. ft capacity, were built in the succeeding 2 years.[73] By 1890 it was evident that the gas companies, like the providers of most other suburban services, were vastly over-extended.

The degree to which the economic collapse of the early 'nineties is attributable to this pattern of extended investment in suburban development is a matter still contested by economic historians.[74] On one side it is argued that the criteria for investment were not those of profitability, that the returns on some investments, particularly in services, were declining substantially in the late 'eighties, that borrowed capital was increasingly diverted to speculation; on the other, it has to be conceded that many service enterprises, particularly those enjoying monopolies, were showing healthy profits at least until 1889-90.[75] Nevertheless, whether as cause or consequence, it is indisputable that the depression of the early 'nineties saw suburban services straitened in just those areas where they had been fully extended in the late 'eighties.

There were signs of difficulty both in the new, outer suburbs where there was evident excess capacity in housing and in inner, working class suburbs where there was heavy unemployment and depopulation. The most substantial declines in population were in South Melbourne, Richmond, Collingwood, Fitzroy and in the City of Melbourne itself. Unemployment and wage reductions, which left men at home or compelled them to economize by walking to work, cut severely into railway and tramway traffic. This decline affected the railways mainly in those inner areas, already well-served by trams, where expansion had been most problematical.

[72] *AIBR*, 16 February 1888, p. 87.

[73] Ibid., 17 February 1890, p. 109 and *Compendium of Lectures*, p. 18. Such prodigious expansion had demanded large increments of capital; between 1884 and 1891 the company made share and debenture issues amounting, in all, to about half a million pounds. (*AIBR*, 13 August 1884, p. 379, 14 August 1886, p. 458, 15 February 1887, p. 85, 16 February 1889, p. 97, 18 August 1891, p. 591.)

[74] The main protagonists are N. G. Butlin, *Investment in Australian Economic Development*, Cambridge 1964, especially Chapters III, IV, and VI and A. R. Hall, *The Stock Exchange of Melbourne and the Victorian Economy*, Canberra 1968, especially Chapter 4.

[75] Compare Butlin, op. cit., pp.414-15 and Hall, op. cit., p. 129.

> Our suburban system, while it pays on the whole, has a great deal of mileage that is shockingly bad in the way of revenue . . . while you get the Brighton line and the Camberwell line, the Essendon line and the Williamstown line, and the line to Caulfield paying very well indeed, you may say that all the rest [i.e. Port Melbourne, Collingwood, Brunswick, St Kilda, Outer Circle] is very poor.[76]

Most sections of the Outer Circle were closed down in the early 'nineties. The railways commissioners' main remedy, however, was to raise fares, grading the increases heavily against first class passengers, periodical ticket holders and outer suburban residents.[77] Some first class passengers announced their intention of henceforth travelling second class; the formation of a 'Second-Class League' enabled them to present a coincidence of individual economies as a gesture of united protest.

> To many, who, like myself, have children attending schools, the proposed addition in fares is a consideration. We have been accustomed to travel first class, and as I am not prepared to acquiesce in the justice of this increased special taxation, we shall certainly join the 'Second-Class League' which it is proposed to form branches of in all the suburbs . . . . [78]

The incidence of the fare increases gave particular offence to periodical ticket holders and those living in 'new towns . . . —such as Canterbury, Surrey Hills, Box Hill, and many other places—which, but for the railway and its facilities would have had no existence'.[79]

The tramways suffered most severe losses on those new, outer routes where they were in competition with the railways. The company's directors explained that trams needed to make about 1*s* a mile before they covered expenses and began to make a profit.

> On lines which pass through closely populated districts, like those of Richmond, Fitzroy, Collingwood and Brunswick, the traffic is sufficient to meet this outlay and yield a handsome surplus, but on lines where large stretches of parkland and other unremunerative areas have to be passed, the same results cannot be looked for. Another disturbing element is the competition offered by the suburban railways, and in the case of the majority of lines this has had an enormous

[76] William Fitzpatrick to Board on Working and Management of the Railways, *VPP* 71/1895, Q. 2052. It would appear, in fact, that the tramways had effectively captured the St Kilda traffic (see ibid., evidence of Lockhead, Q. 1365, and compare traffic figures cited above, p. 337). The Reports of the Railways Commissioners for the mid-'nineties do not furnish traffic figures, merely revenue.

[77] *Argus*, 6 May 1892, p. 4H (editorial).

[78] 'Second Class Leaguer' in *Argus*, 6 May 1892, p. 6. One passenger with a family of 8 estimated that he paid £45 per annum for fares and could cut that amount by two-thirds by moving closer to the centre of town.

[79] Ibid.

> effect in reducing the traffic. The result of the past year has been that on some lines the return per tram mile has been under 9d when about 1*s* was required to pay expenses. The West Melbourne line has been run at a considerable loss, and neither the Port Melbourne, South Melbourne, nor Toorak lines have paid expenses. The Prahran line has yielded a slight profit, but the line to St Kilda has not quite paid its way. The horse lines to Kew and Hawthorn are worked at a loss.[80]

There was also cutting competition from cabmen.[81] By 1894-5 the average return over *all* lines was less than a shilling a mile.[82] Employees' salaries were drastically cut and trams were run at 12 m.p.h. instead of 9 m.p.h. so that fewer cars could make the same number of trips.[83] In 1893 it was suggested that less profitable routes might be abandoned;[84] but the company, perhaps under pressure from the trust, maintained its services throughout the depression.

Gas companies, like other suburban services, were saddled with enormous excess capacity. From 1891-2 there was a steep decline in consumption[85] which, in the case of the Metropolitan Gas Company, fell from 1,898,250,000 cu. ft in the period 1883-91 to 983,740,000 cu. ft in 1891-8. Suppliers suffered from the competition of other illuminants especially electricity which, by 1894, was being used for street lighting in the City of Melbourne, Richmond, Essendon, Collingwood, Hawthorn, and South Yarra.[86] Gas consumption for cooking and heating also fell away. By 1894 the Metropolitan Gas Company had repossessed 6,233 gas stoves—about half of those on loan in 1890.[87]

The 1880s saw the reconstruction of Melbourne upon a new urban plan. The socio-spatial patterns, transport networks and essential services which were laid down in those years served the city, with little alteration or addition, for another generation, and are easily recognized even today. Indeed, so ample was the provision of services in those years that, for a decade or more, their providers had to bear the costs of enormous unused capacity.

80 *Argus*, 4 July 1891.
81 *AIBR*, 17 August 1893, p. 788.
82 *Journal of Commerce*, 9 April 1895, p. 6, 21 May 1895, p. 6.
83 By August 1894 salaries had been cut by 45 per cent at the higher levels, 35 per cent in the middle ranks, and 25 per cent on the lowest rungs. Salaries below 30*s* were left unchanged. (*AIBR*, 18 August 1894, p. 551); *Australasian Ironmonger*, 1 August 1893, p. 229.
84 *Age*, 10 February 1893, p. 6G.
85 *AIBR*, 18 February 1892, p. 121.
86 H.U. Alcock Electric Light Company began operations in 1890. *Australasian Ironmonger*, 1 February 1891, p. 55, 1 May 1891, pp. 129, 144, 1 June 1891, p. 174, 1 October 1891, p. 399.
87 C. H. Eddey, *Compendium of Lectures*, p. 48.

M. T. Daly

THE DEVELOPMENT OF THE URBAN PATTERN OF NEWCASTLE

Economists and geographers interested in the internal structure and development of cities have produced few general models explaining the processes governing land use distributions. The first, and most enduring hypothesis, is the economic rent model in which competing land uses are distributed to different locations according to their rent-earning capacities; when it is assumed that the central business district is the most desirable location, a gradation of land uses, distinguished by type and intensity of use, takes place from the centre of the city and gives rise to a concentric pattern of uses. The idea was first put forward by the American economist, Haig,[1] in 1926 when cities were relatively more compact than today; when motor transport and rapid transit systems were only just beginning to recast the shape of cities. Minor modifications were made by Hoyt[2] in the 1930s (to accommodate sectoral growth along highways and other features) and in the 1940s by Harris and Ullman[3] (to take into account regional growth centres within the city). In the 1950s and early 1960s Haig's basic equilibrium model was revived in more sophisticated form by Alonso[4] and Muth.[5]

It is instructive that the major efforts have gone into the construction of static models whereas, as Dickinson[6] points out, 'even a strict economic interpretation of a city's function requires a historical evaluation'. Recently, Garrison[7] and Morrill[8] have attempted to place a temporal

[1] R. M. Haig, 'Toward an Understanding of the Metropolis', *Quarterly Journal of Economics*, Vol. 40 (1926), pp. 179-208; 402-34.

[2] H. Hoyt, 'The Pattern of Movement in Residential Rent Neighbourhoods' in *Readings in Urban Geography*, eds H. F. Mayer and C. F. Kohn, Chicago 1959, pp. 499-510.

[3] C. Harris, E. Ullman, 'The Nature of Cities' in *Readings in Urban Geography*, eds H. F. Mayer and C. F. Kohn, Chicago 1959, pp. 277-86.

[4] W. Alonso, *Location and Land Use*, Cambridge, Mass. 1964.

[5] R. Muth, 'The Spatial Structure of the Housing Market', *PapProcRegSciAssoc*, Vol. 7 (1961), pp. 207-20.

[6] R. E. Dickinson, 'The City of History', *Annals of Association of American Geographers*, Vol. 52 (1962), p. 300.

[7] W. L. Garrison, 'Toward Simulation Models of Urban Growth and Development', *Proceedings of I.G.U. Symposium in Urban Geography, Lund 1960*, ed. K. Norborg, Lund 1962, pp. 91-108.

[8] R. Morrill, 'Expansion of the Urban Fringe: A Simulation Experiment', *PapProcRegSciAssoc*, Vol. 15 (1965), pp. 185-99.

dimension in urban studies by means of simulation experiments. Blumenfeld,[9] building on the general principles underlying the economic rent-accessibility hypotheses, has argued that cities expand areally in waves from a dominant centre. The crest of the wave corresponds to the fastest-growing zone at any time period, and it advances outward at a fairly uniform rate. However, the size and distribution of suburban centres in Newcastle, and the subsequent land use pattern, indicate that forces other than those proposed by Haig and Blumenfeld have been active in determining the growth of the city.

Newcastle's growth has largely involved conurbation, by which a number of once independent towns have been subsumed. Many of the suburbs were once mining towns and their distribution throughout modern metropolitan Newcastle follows the scatter of coal seams rather than the dictates of the modified rent models (Map 1). The location and dominance of the central business district in Newcastle has largely depended on the importance of the port in the regional and national economy. A transport system linking the mining towns to the port was built up because of the necessity to ship coal won from the local mines. A flow of agricultural goods from Newcastle's hinterland enhanced the status of the port and helped to expand the importance of the commercial area which grew up around the docks. Before the advent of rail transport the port provided the principal means of contact between Newcastle and the outside world; the coming of the railway meant only increased flows of goods to the port of Newcastle, and a more vigorous growth for its commercial and administrative adjuncts. The diversity of enterprises carried on in Newcastle strengthened the town economically, and enabled it to weather the various economic climes better than the scattered towns throughout the coalfields (even though some of these rivalled Newcastle for population in the mid-nineteenth century). Consequently, Newcastle grew more rapidly than the coal towns and, as marketable coal reserves dwindled and transport systems improved, it subsumed many of them. With the advent of large-scale industry in the twentieth century most factories were located close to the port in the inner suburbs of Newcastle, reinforcing the dominance of the central area. The process of development has left modern Newcastle with a settlement pattern which represents a major departure from the simple models mentioned above;[10] the historical forces shaping Newcastle's growth therefore bear closer investigation.

9 H. Blumenfeld, 'Are Land Patterns Predictable?', *Journal of the Amer. Institute of Planners*, Vol. 25 (1959), p. 63.

10 A detailed study of the difference between Newcastle's growth and the model explanations is presented in M. Daly, *Land Use of the Newcastle and Lake Macquarie Regions*, The Hunter Valley Research Foundation, Maryville, 1967.

Growth of the port and the central business district (CBD)

As outlined above, the port and the commercial heart of Newcastle have been the prime factors in promoting the town to dominance over the other centres in the district. The Hunter Valley was discovered by Lieutenant Shortland on 9 September 1797 and in 1801 a penal settlement, dependent on the workings of the local coal deposits, was established. The village, set on the estuary of the Hunter River, vacillated between stagnation and absolute decline for two decades, until the prisoners were removed to Port Macquarie in 1822 and the settlement was declared a free town. Surveyor Dangar designed and laid out the township in 1823 and established the site of the present business centre, basing his choice on the location of the military barracks, the likely encroachments of the nearby sandhills and proximity to the wharf. The removal of the penal character from the settlement induced the first notable influx of free settlers, although the population remained fairly static rising from 1,169 in 1821 to 1,377 in 1841 as free settlers replaced convicts.

Agriculture in the Hunter Valley flourished after 1823, especially in the Wallis Plains area; the port town for the district was not Newcastle but Morpeth, at the navigable head of the river, the natural outlet for the Valley's goods. The triad of East and West Maitland and Morpeth formed the urban commercial centre of the district. The poverty of the land around Newcastle for agricultural purposes mitigated against the town's growth.

A major fillip came to Newcastle, which in 1829 had covered an area of little more than one square mile, when on 13 June 1831 the steamer *Sophia Jane* began its voyages, dramatically bringing the town into closer contact with Sydney. Newcastle was 145 miles away from Sydney by the Wiseman's Ferry-Broken Back Mountain road, but the advent of the steamship meant relatively swift transport of goods and passengers between the two towns. It significantly enhanced the status of the port of Newcastle.

On 30 March 1857 Sir William Dennison opened the Newcastle-Maitland railway tapping the agricultural wealth of the Hunter Valley, boosting trade in the port of Newcastle and bringing about the eclipse of the Maitland complex as the commercial heart of the Valley; agricultural goods could be brought more quickly and economically to Newcastle by rail for shipment to their markets. An adequate rail terminus was provided at Newcastle and some much needed improvements to port facilities were carried out. The increased standing of Newcastle in the Hunter Valley region was reflected in commercial buoyancy and a relatively large population: in 1851 there were 1,340 persons in Newcastle,[11] compared with only 335 in the neighbouring colliery villages.

The vibrant growth of mining around Newcastle in the 1860s caused the 1861 population of 3,562 to double in a decade, provided added trade for the port of Newcastle, and promoted growth in its commercial row.[12] When in 1871 the population of Newcastle reached 7,124 the town dominated the other urban centres in the district. A busy port and rising land values complemented an impressive commercial centre: 'Hunter Street here is, in many respects, equal to George Street, Sydney'.[13]

Newcastle's ascendancy as a regional port was the principal cause, outside of coal mining, for the town's continued expansion. The growing hinterland of the port was reflected in an increasing diversification of commercial activities in Newcastle, which provided a decisive boost to the established Hunter Street business district. A strong element in the predominance of Hunter Street over other commercial centres on the coalfield was the significance of Newcastle as a regional capital. Newcastle's population grew with the increasing complexity of its functions, and its growing regional and state importance, to reach 8,986 in 1881.

At the start of the twentieth century the business centre for the rapidly expanding city of Newcastle was firmly established in Hunter Street, close to the port and major rail terminus. Two of the primary reasons for the importance of Hunter Street above the business districts of the coal towns were the early founding of Newcastle, and the considerable influence of the port on the growth of the city. A third can be found in the coal trade.

Coal Mining

> As regards Newcastle it is essentially a seaport and a coally seaport . . . every third house sells slops or ropes or blocks or some of the many other articles required by those who go down to the sea in ships. Whilst if you pass three persons talking together you will be sure to hear that their conservation is about coals.[14]

The growth of the port of Newcastle, and of the commercial district which surrounded it, was indissolubly linked with the coal trade.

[11] H. W. H. King, *The Urban Pattern of the Hunter Valley*, The Hunter Valley Research Foundation, Maryville, 1963, p. 32.

[12] 'A wonderful change has come over Newcastle since I last visited it some eight or nine years ago and when I denounced it as the Sleepy Hollow of New South Wales. . . . Coals have had the effect of making Newcastle a lively business centre.' *Sydney Morning Herald*, 23 April 1866.

[13] *Sydney Mail*, 23 February 1878, p. 10.

[14] *Sydney Morning Herald*, 20 August 1866, p. 4.

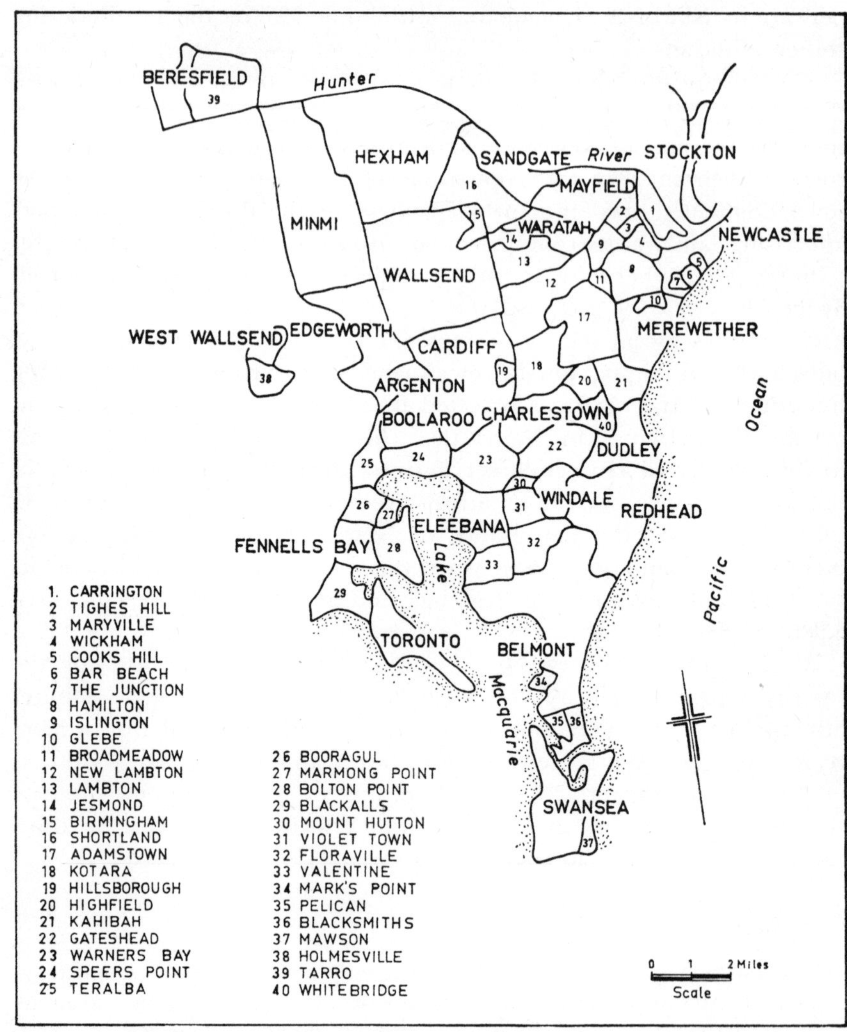

Map 1—LOCATION MAP OF NEWCASTLE AND SUBURBS

Traders visited Newcastle soon after Shortland's discovery of the river and coal was being shipped to Bengal as early as 1799.[15] In 1801 Governor King surveyed the coal deposits and declared them Crown property. The earliest shafts were sunk close to the wharves, and coal shipments provided the bulk of the outgoing cargo from the port between 1800 and 1822.

[15] F. A. Cadell, 'A Survey of Newcastle from the First Settlement to the Present Day', *RAHSJP*, Vol. 22 (1936), p. 378.

The small town of Newcastle was saved from decline in its immediate post-convict days by the activities of the Australian Agricultural Company (AA Company) which was founded in London on 18 January 1823.[16] In 1829 the AA Company directed its attentions to the mineral deposits of Newcastle, where it was granted a lease of the colliery rights for a period of 31 years. The old government shafts were found to be useless and a new pit, tapping the rich Borehole seam, was sunk close to the river and a half mile west of the settlement around the wharf. The coal industry assumed a new efficiency, with production lifting from 780 tons in 1829 to 4,000 tons in 1830 and in a further decade to 30,265 tons.

The proximity of the first commercial coal mines to the wharves coincided with the commencement of regular steamship services to Newcastle, so that the increased activity in and around the port firmly established the locality of the town's business centre. As other mining towns grew, Newcastle maintained a natural hegemony, gained not only from its earlier founding and its diversified activities, but also from the fact that most mining companies set up their headquarters close to each other in the business heart of Hunter Street.

By the end of the 1830s the AA Company had placed the coal mining industry in Newcastle on a solid commercial base and this had provoked criticism of its monopoly over the coal leases. By 1845 new mines, opened in defiance of the AA Company, were producing enough coal to spark a protest; the AA Company, after a court dispute, agreed to relinquish the monopoly in 1850 in exchange for the title deeds of its land grant in Newcastle. The move had two implications for the future residential growth of Newcastle. Firstly, in the decade following the removal of the coal monopoly, production jumped by almost 70,000 tons to 94,631 tons[17] and settlement burst the confines to which it had been held in its government and early monopolistic days. The foundations of the suburbs of Newcastle were laid. Secondly, the control of large areas of urban land were vested in the hands of one company and, as such investiture was repeated in the interests of other companies in subsequent years, it helped to lay the basis of the nucleated land use pattern which is apparent in modern Newcastle.

Following the dictates of the coal seams, mining establishments tended to successively ring Newcastle at different stages of its history. Some modified 'crest of the wave' elements may be discerned in the

[16] The company included in its ranks the British Attorney-General; the British Solicitor-General; 28 members of Parliament; the Governor, the Deputy Governor and five directors of the East India Company. See H. W. H. Huntington, 'History of Newcastle', *Newcastle Morning Herald*, 10 August 1897, p. 5.

[17] J. Jervis, 'The Rise of Newcastle', *RAHSJP*, Vol. 21 (1935), p. 181.

pattern of growth because, in proportion to the commercial and industrial complexity of Newcastle, the size of its accompanying population, and advances in the means of transport, each ring of independent colliery towns was subsumed by the city. However, the size and siting of the urban nodes, and the areas of unused land within the city boundaries, were results of the mining activities; they did not follow the suggested 'normal' distribution of people and functions.

The first ring of colliery towns: the 1840s

The foundation of the first ring of settlements came in the 1840s. In 1842 and in 1848 the AA Company sank two pits, a mile to the south of Newcastle, giving rise to the Lake Macquarie Road settlement, which formed the nucleus of the suburb of Cook's Hill. A series of tunnels on Dr Mitchell's estate, four miles south of Newcastle, gave rise to a mining village which marked the beginnings of Merewether. The AA Company initiated a further mine during the decade, opening up a part of the Hamilton area to develop more of the Borehole seam. Hamilton was to become one of the largest mining towns in New South Wales. Accessibility to work dominated residential site selection. The miners were, in the main, poor immigrants or released convicts, and the long hours they worked, coupled with poor communications, forced them to live in unpainted, impoverished dwellings close to the pit head.

The growth of the colliery villages was slow and in 1851 they had only 335 inhabitants. The opening of two pits by the AA Company at Cook's Hill and Hamilton,[18] and the transportation of English miners to the field, helped to prevent an actual decline in the coalfields, following an outflow of workers to the gold strikes in the 1850s. In contrast, Newcastle benefited from better port facilities and rail connections, to maintain a steady rate of growth (an extra 2,222 persons 1851-61) and a clear dominance over other towns in the area. Waratah was the only coal town to be founded in the 1850s. A hill, six miles west of Newcastle, caused delays in the construction of the Newcastle-Maitland railway, and a camp was established whilst the difficulties were negotiated. The camp grew into a township when an excellent seam of Borehole coal was discovered, and the Waratah Coal Company began operations in 1859. The principal components of the first ring of colliery towns around Newcastle were established.

[18] Hamilton was at that time known as Pittown.

The 1860s and 1870s

The 1860s were a boom period for coal mining in Newcastle. Of the four companies operating at Waratah, the largest, the Waratah Coal Company, purchased 142 acres of land on the river front,[19] installed coal-loading facilities and connecting train lines, and greatly extended the size and scope of the port. A new pit was opened in Hamilton[20] helping to increase the population and extent of the town. The competition from the large companies working the Borehole seams forced the small Merewether mines to close, and the group of colliery villages turned to Newcastle as a source of employment. The first signs of suburbanization were evident.

As some places in the first ring of colliery villages began to lose their independence to Newcastle, a second ring of coal towns was established (see Maps 2 and 3). At Lambton, six miles west of Newcastle, new mines were opened by the Scottish Australian Company in 1861 and by the Alnwick Company in 1862; the town site was surveyed also in 1862. The new mines flourished: the Lambton output of 182,007 tons in 1867 was a record for an Australian colliery and by that time there were 400 people in the town. In 1867 a pit was opened at New Lambton, giving rise to another township. The third, and most important, of the second ring of colliery towns was Wallsend. In 1860 the Newcastle and Wallsend Coal Company laid out a township around their new pit, and in 1862 the Co-Operative Miners Association built an adjoining town, Plattsburg, giving rise to the most prosperous of the colliery urban centres.

Scattered developments to the south of Newcastle promoted the growth of small villages which would eventually form part of the city. The mining hamlets which sprang up at Cardiff, Teralba and Boolaroo were to retain their independence longer than the Wallsend-Lambton group, and their eventual suburbanization marked a third stage in the growth of Newcastle.

The 1870s saw the peak of independent development for the coal towns. Their combined population was 9,000 in 1871 and six towns gained municipal status in the decade. The general buoyancy of the coal industry stimulated growth in the inner towns (Waratah: population 1,850, 1879; Hamilton: population 2,000, 1879; Merewether: population 1,240, 1879); this was complemented by developments in the second ring of colliery towns which included Lambton, New Lambton and Adamstown and which was dominated by Wallsend-Plattsburg which reached a population of 5,000 by the end of the decade.

[19] The area became known as Port Waratah and covered much of the land now occupied by BHP.

[20] On the site of the present Newcastle racecourse.

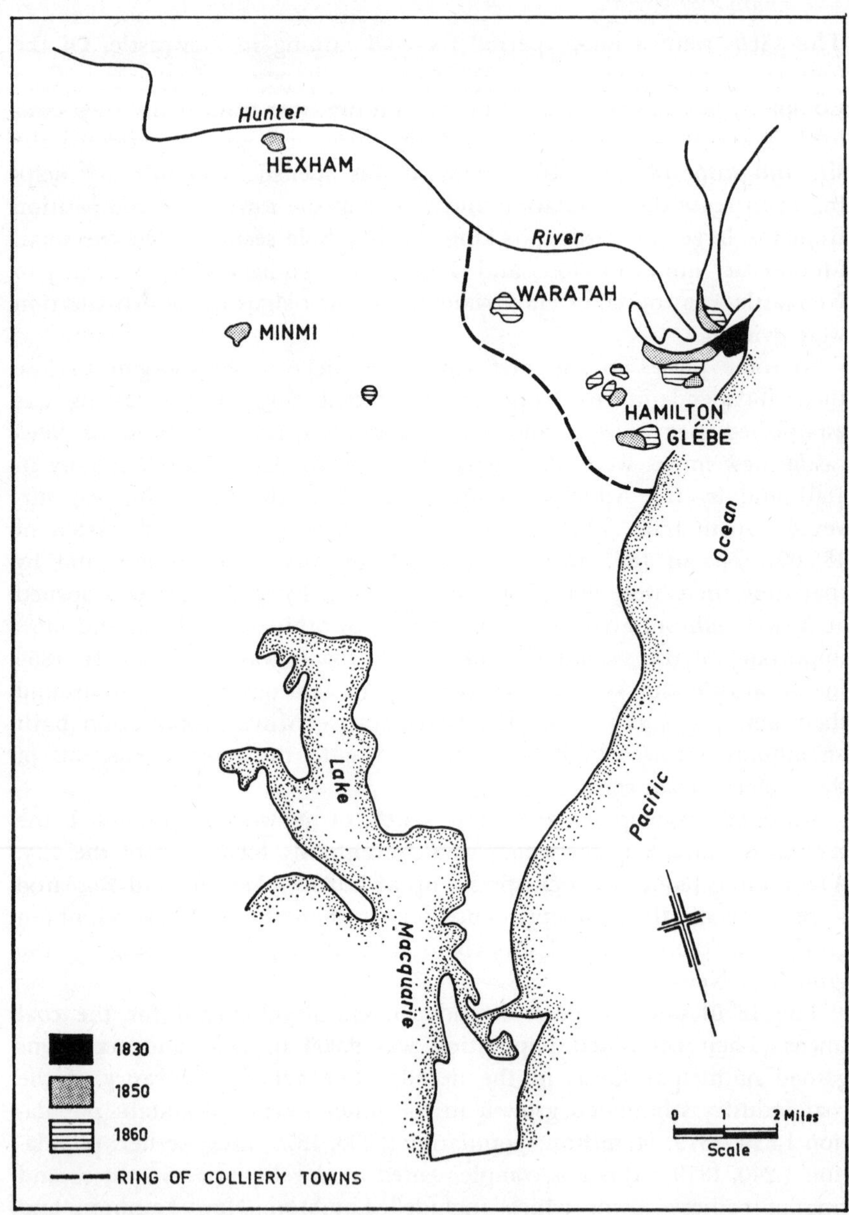

Map 2—Historical Development of Newcastle Built-up Areas 1830, 1850, 1860

The change after 1880

The pattern of growth on the coalfield changed abruptly after 1880. The combined population of the colliery towns had climbed to 15,000 in 1881, although the area had passed through a period of depression which caused the prophets of doom to predict that 'the present centre of mining life where the hum of business source never ceases, will probably in the course of a few years become deserted villages'.[21] However, communications had improved to the point where a twice-daily coaching service ran from the city to Wallsend-Plattsburg via Tighes Hill, Waratah and Lambton (although fares were not cheap in relation to wages). More importantly, the Government Inspector of Tramways visited Newcastle in 1880 and supported a system of tramways to connect the mining villages to the city. On 18 September 1886 work commenced, and 18 months later the first tram ran from Newcastle to Plattsburg. The improving transport system complemented a changing economic base in Newcastle, so that the decline in the local economies of the coal towns was balanced by a rise in the degree of their dependence on Newcastle. Suburbanization prevented the absolute decline of the towns. Hamilton, Wickham, Stockton and Merewether[22] were all indisputably suburban in character by 1890.

In the 1880s Waratah, Lambton, New Lambton and Adamstown passed through a transitory stage between complete independence and complete suburbanization. The invigorating factor in the growth of the municipalities, which had a combined population of 5,300 persons in 1885, was the coal industry; however, as each advanced towards suburban status it divested itself of the singularly coal-centred aspects by introducing a degree of manufacturing and commercial activity; added to the improved transport network, these helped to bring the towns into closer unison with Newcastle, and to effect a suburban character.

Throughout the 1890s and 1900s the process of transforming the second ring of colliery towns into suburbs was completed. Prior to 1880 the subsuming of nearby colliery towns by Newcastle had been gradual, but the discovery of the South Maitland coalfield by Sir Edgeworth David in 1885-6 brought an abrupt shift in emphasis in the mining industry, and necessitated a change in the economic bases of the colliery towns. Continued growth in the commercial heart of Newcastle, and the sudden rise in industrial employment opportunities in the Port Waratah area, stabilized the position and, by 1920, the once-colliery towns, enveloped by a line from Wallsend to Adamstown, prospered as suburbs of Newcastle (Map 4).

21 *Newcastle Despatch*, 13 November 1880, p. 2.
22 Merewether was proclaimed a municipality on 30 August 1885.

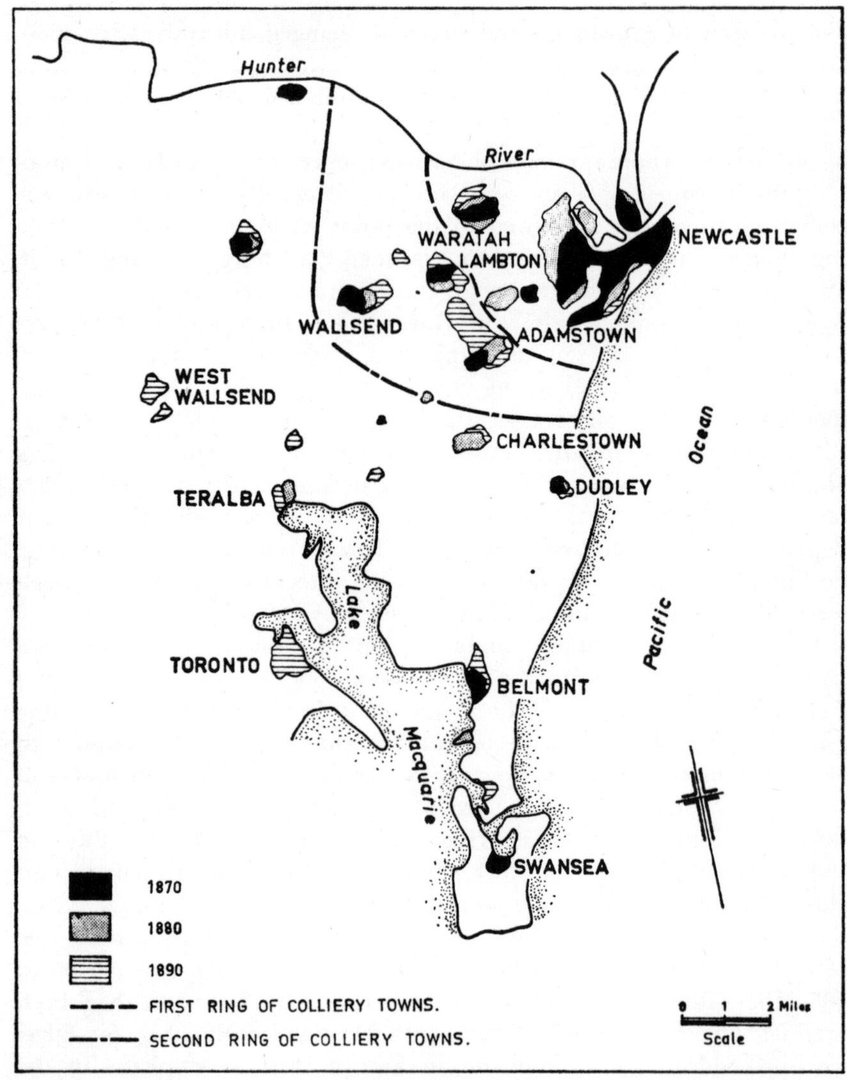

Map 3—Historical Development of Newcastle Built-up Areas 1870, 1880, 1890

Industry

While coal mining, and the trade flows and commercial activities associated with it, explain the location, size and fluctuating fortunes of many Newcastle suburbs, recognition must be given to other forces which have played a part in forming the residential areas of the city. Secondary industry is one such force.

Industrial undertakings continually added to the diversity of Newcastle's economy. The first successful factories in the town date back to 1838 when two salt works and two mills for grinding grain were operating. Many of the earliest factories were located in the Merewether group of towns, south of Newcastle: the Newcastle Coal and Copper Company began producing coke in 1855, providing some employment for displaced miners; a large pottery works, opened in 1865, stimulated the growth of a small village, called the Pottery, the forerunner of the modern Bar Beach suburb. Secondary industry was also important in the Waratah area, where pottery works were established in 1865 and followed, in 1866, by the opening of the Newcastle Gas Company, and in 1867 by the erection of the smelting works of the Wallaroo and Moonta Copper Mining Company.[23] Although coal mining was the major activity carried on in Waratah in the 1870s, the addition of a sawmill, a pottery works, a brick-making concern and quarries to the industrial base of the previous decade, represented important stimuli to growth. In 1872 the English and Australian Copper Smelting Works were opened, and the settlement which grew up around it was the nucleus of the suburb of Georgetown.

Secondary industry in the nineteenth century sparked the formation of some embryonic suburbs and stabilized the economies of others, but in no way did it play a decisive part in the creation of the city of Newcastle. The twentieth century brought a change; on 2 June 1915 the Broken Hill Proprietary Company (BHP Company) established a steelworks in Newcastle. The move was significant for the Australian as well as the local economy and had a profound effect on the growth of the city.

The choice of Newcastle as the site for the venture, based primarily on the advantages of coal deposits close to the port, raised the city to national importance, and introduced stability and vibrant growth into the local economy. It concentrated employment opportunities into an area close to the port and the CBD, and provided alternative work for the inhabitants of the former mining towns. Tramcars, trains, bicycles, and latterly motor cars, helped to release the worker from the strict ties of residence to workplace, and completed the transformation of mining towns into a definite cortège of suburbs around Newcastle. The population of Newcastle and its suburbs reached 88,095 in 1921, with 16,330 people resident in the city and a further 72,000 spread about the 13 suburbs which encircled it.

[23] This was the first major industrial undertaking in Newcastle which depended upon imported raw materials; copper ore was shipped from Port Adelaide.

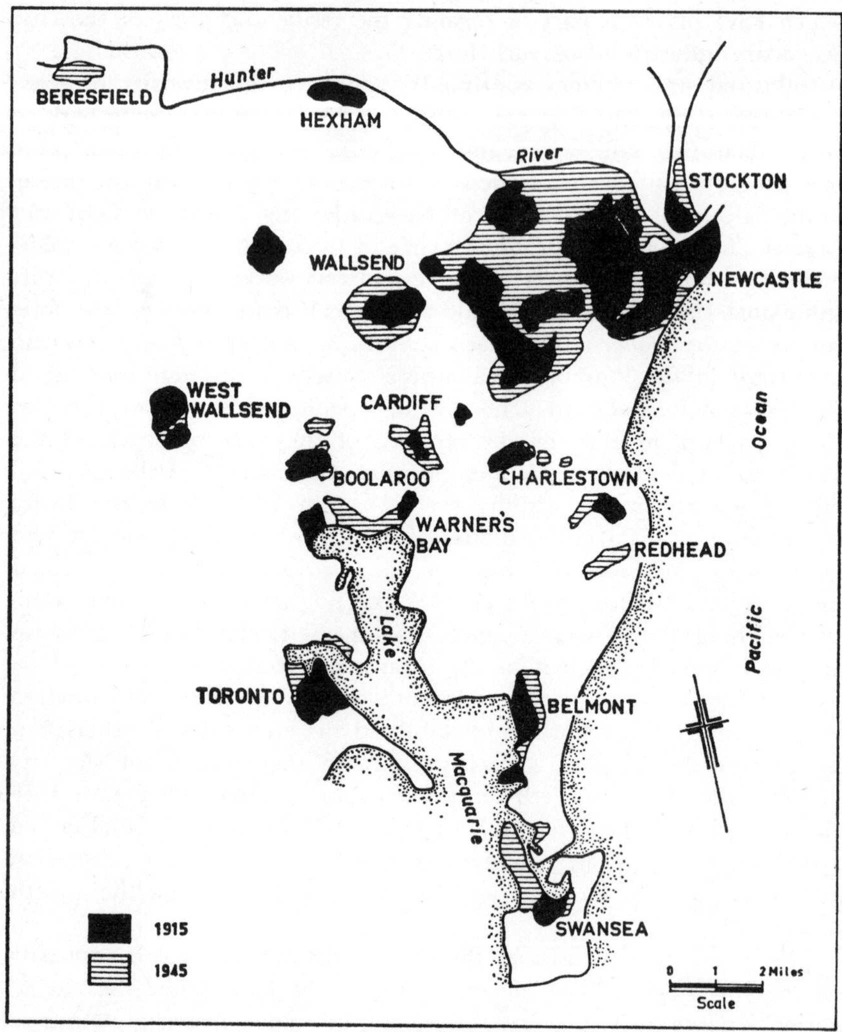

Map 4—Historical Development of Newcastle Built-up Areas 1915, 1945

The production of basic steel in Newcastle invited the establishment of large steel-processing and engineering plants in the city, and in quick succession Commonwealth Steel, Lysaghts, Stewart and Lloyds, Rylands, and Goninans, were associated with BHP[24] in making New-

[24] Although some of these companies independently established in Newcastle, their shares were soon controlled by BHP following a vigorous policy of vertical integration initiated by Essington Lewis, chief executive of the Company from 1921. Goninans was the exception.

castle a substantial industrial centre. The industries in the Port Waratah area employed over 10,000 men in 1921; the industrial area and the relatively proximate CBD (proximate in relation to the growing overall size of Newcastle) formed a pivotal point for the growth of the city. If the central area provided direction for the employment and business interests of the inhabitants of Newcastle, the former towns still provided nodes for residential growth. Local loyalties and interests, and the provision of urban services, enticed many people to settle in the erstwhile colliery centres, promoting urban growth which has given Newcastle its typical multiple-nucleated pattern.

General location factors

Space does not permit a discussion of the multiplicity of other factors which have shaped Newcastle's growth. Important among these are the tourist origins of many lakeside suburbs, the effect of improving communications and local entrepreneurship on local growth, the provision of local government services in certain areas, and the all-important extra-regional economic forces. However, the major influences on the development of the city have been highlighted.

The particularities of Newcastle's growth serve to illustrate the inadequacies of the highly simplified general theories so far developed to explain internal city growth and structure. Elsewhere[25] it has been shown that the pattern of development in Newcastle is replicated in many other places and the so-called 'dispersed city hypothesis' has been suggested as a general formulation of the process. The study provides an interesting picture of the development of one of Australia's major industrial cities and demonstrates, to a point, the usefulness of historical studies to an understanding of modern city land use distributions.

[25] M. Daly, 'The Lower Hunter Valley Urban Complex and the Dispersed City Hypothesis', *The Aust. Geographer*, Vol. X (1968), pp. 472-82.

Weston Bate

THE URBAN SPRINKLE: COUNTRY TOWNS AND AUSTRALIAN REGIONAL HISTORY

'The country township is the forgotten feature of the frontier.' Thus begins a seminal chapter in D. W. Meinig's *On the Margins of the Good Earth*, the most systematic contribution, so far, to the writing of regional history in Australia.[1] Meinig's task was simplified by the homogeneity of his region (the South Australian wheatlands) as well as by the initial success and later wide extension of settlement, and by the lack of political and social complications such as bedevilled selection in the eastern colonies. But that must not be allowed to mask the fact that the author's training as a geographer and his experience in a similar research field in the United States gave him an advantage over other pioneer regional historians in Australia.

Regional history without some geography is a boat without a rudder. And regional urban history, in particular, depends upon at least a substructure of geographical concepts such as town hinterlands, transport networks, service categories and land use patterns. In this connection it is instructive to observe the contrast between Meinig's maps and those in other regional histories, and to notice that in his text (on p. 173, for instance) there is a resultant clarity of exposition. He moves easily from detail to generalization, and back again, because he has a firm inductive structure. This contrasts with a tendency of other historians to write up the highlights of individual towns without worrying about wider significance or inner coherence.

On the modest bookshelf of Australian regional history, there are naturally important works in which the influence of geography and the emphasis on towns is almost negligible. Margaret Kiddle's *Men of Yesterday*[2] and Geoffrey Bolton's *A Thousand Miles Away*[3] are prime examples. They represent the traditional historical approach. Bolton has no generalized treatment of towns. They are mentioned sporadically in his work, and they wax and wane in a limited context. For instance, he runs a lively urban premiership race on the North Queensland

[1] London 1963, Chapter VIII.
[2] *A Social History of the Western District of Victoria 1834-1890*, Melbourne 1961.
[3] *A History of North Queensland to 1920*, Brisbane 1963.

coast (with Townsville victorious) but does not establish the towns in a wider pattern. He is obviously interested in their character, and he gives some fascinating descriptions of their ethos and development, but the criteria tend to be shallow. His material is limited to population figures, local politics, businesses, schools, churches and leading citizens. He seeks far more coherence for gold mining, sugar planting, the Kanaka question and politics than for urban affairs.

It is much the same with Margaret Kiddle's fine study. Although she devotes a separate chapter to the towns of the Western District, it is set apart from the core of her work. In dealing with individual towns her treatment is even more descriptive than Bolton's, for it is based largely on the accounts of visitors like Anthony Trollope and Julian Thomas ('The Vagabond'); and although that part of the chapter is followed by a sensitive review of town activities in general, the impression given is that to Margaret Kiddle the towns were interesting but not really important. She may have felt that to treat them more seriously, say by reconstructing their economies (as she does, in a way, for the pastoralists) or to search out their ethos (as she does for pastoralists, selectors, and Aborigines) would have interrupted her great theme about the transformation of the pioneering generation and their world.[4] By cutting the towns off from the countryside, the focus is kept on rural matters and on men like Niel Black.

In the interests of accuracy, however, the towns should have been written larger. And that could have been done without threatening Margaret Kiddle's theme. Indeed to have established the role of towns in the rural economy might have strengthened rather than weakened it. Without the markets of the gold towns, wool was a lame staple, cattle only moderately profitable and horses a sideline. It could be said that by injecting confidence into the rural sector of the economy, and by establishing a compelling picture of progress, the booming towns of the 1860s were responsible for the willingness of squatters to go into debt to buy land—just as it is possible to argue that it was the failure of town populations to grow in the 'seventies, rather than the amount of land that the squatters purchased, that undid them.

Quite apart from that point, a study of the hinterland of a gold town like Ballarat reveals the successful development of farming in the 1850s on blocks of eighty acres and less, which was a prototype of selection.[5] At the same time, the timber needs of the town and its mines supported numerous steam sawmills, which helped to clear the

[4] Possibly it was just as much a matter of time. See R. M. Crawford's note on Margaret Kiddle, *Men of Yesterday*, pp. ix-xii.

[5] Map, *County Lands, Parish of Warrenheip, County of Grant*, lithographed 31 December 1858.

country for miles around. This added to the capacity of an engineering industry, which, while retaining its original base in goldmining equipment, diversified into locomotives, milling and farming machinery and made it practicable to use steam power on farms years (if not decades) before it would otherwise have been achieved. In and around the gold towns, therefore, there were forces destructive to pastoral interests and traditions. They were expressed politically in demands to legalize mining on private property and for selection and protection. Nowhere in Victoria was this so cogent a trilogy as at Ballarat, in the very Western District which was also the stronghold of squatter interests. The towns represented flexible and adventurous investment at a time when the squatter's adventurous phase was often behind him.

If she had looked more deeply into the life of the towns, Margaret Kiddle might have been impressed with the pervasiveness of their influence in the district. According to size, they provided hospitals, benevolent asylums, schools and markets, which all served wide hinterlands—over a hundred miles to the west in the case of Ballarat. Their dealers in fodder and stock, their investors and in some cases their brokers, their politicans, Orange Lodges, Mechanics Institutes, Agricultural and Pastoral Shows, their branches of the Supreme Court, gaols, brothels, hotels, foundries, their contractors, lawyers, architects, builders, accountants, retailers and hawkers were all part of a reservoir of services, skills and attitudes which filled the land with new voices, different hopes, enlarged conceptions.

Just how far and how quickly the urban ethos penetrated the pastoral hearth can be measured in the history of towns like Colac, recently the subject of an MA thesis at Melbourne University.[6] Here, by the 'sixties the urban ganglion could be clearly distinguished from its pastoral setting. It was linked along strengthening lines of communication to larger urban structures in the colony and overseas. Pastoralists, and institutions in which they believed, gradually mattered less and less in town life. Among the churches, for instance, Wesleyans and Roman Catholics grew rapidly relative to Presbyterians and Anglicans. Political reformers drew inspiration and funds from Melbourne, and Ballarat was seen as a great ally in developing Colac's hinterland in the Otway Ranges. Further away, Hamilton was a different kind of town, insulated by distance from the influence of Melbourne and the goldfields. It is one of three quite different towns whose development in relation to their hinterlands is the subject of a recent urban study.[7] Just how

[6] G. C. Evans, *A Social History of Colac, 1860-1900*.

[7] J. M. Richmond, *Country Town Growth in South-East Australia: Three Regional Studies 1861-1891*, PhD thesis, Australian National University, 1969.

different it was from other towns in its region can only be discovered as similar work of a rigorous nature and with common criteria is undertaken. In the meantime, though, it is clear that in terms of urban history the Western District was far from homogeneous.

Mature studies of a single town within its district are rare. Susan Priestley's *Echuca* (Brisbane 1965) and *Warracknabeal* (Brisbane 1967) and Yvonne Palmer's *Track of the Years* (a history of St Arnaud, Melbourne 1955) are among the best. They not only demonstrate how varied urban development was but they also point to its complexity, and to the important role of townsmen in rural development. These rather than regional histories seem to provide the best opportunity to study the financing of agricultural expansion and the marketing of its produce. Indeed they may contain the only real clues to it.

What has just been said about the complexity of urban organization and experience will help to explain why at this stage in Australian historiography regional studies are weaker in handling towns than rural affairs. A few observations or statistics about a squatting station can be added quite simply to others of the same kind. The level of sophistication is low. But similar random observations about a town (and they sometimes pass as history) are potentially misleading. The life of a town is embodied in the interaction of hundreds of different interests, involving thousands of people and numerous institutions. The life of a pastoral estate represents few interactions, few people and an hierarchical organization, the pulse of which can be felt by examining (in contrast to the town) a mere handful of records. Conceptually simple, geographically well-defined and historically uncomplicated, the squatting runs of a whole district can be represented fairly convincingly, as Margaret Kiddle has shown, in the documents deposited by half a dozen men. But a single year of the newspaper of a one-paper town could amount to as much. Small wonder then that regional history has been told essentially in terms of rural events, often the black and white drama of farmer versus pastoralist.

By contrast, in *Squatter, Selector, and Storekeeper* (Sydney 1968) Duncan Waterson makes the towns loom large. They are seen almost as bogeymen or foreigners on the Darling Downs, doing-in the squatters politically and often doing-in the selectors economically. This view, despite its value, seems incipiently anti-urban. Dr Waterson surely exaggerates the materialism of the townsmen. He borrows D. W. A. Baker's interpretation of the Robertson Land Acts of New South Wales and suggests that townsmen wanted agricultural settlement rather less than they wanted to strike a political blow at the squatters.[8] My

[8] P. 106. Waterson might usefully have distinguished more lucidly between country town and capital city when talking about urban bourgeoisie. His assumption

quarrel with him here is not that he indicts the towns for materialism. He is rare among Australian historians in seeing the value of insights into an urban ethos. It is just that he does not explore, let alone prove his point. Instead, he deduces, apparently from Marxism, that men who were making money were insensitive to the needs of their fellow men, from whom they were insulated by class stratification, which he sees, however, as by no means hardened.[9] Under this regimen, the construction of town halls, churches, hospitals and other community facilities is seen almost as a fetish. Toowoomba is especially distrusted, for it was the largest and wealthiest of the towns.

What Dr Waterson says may be true. Yet it is presented at such a high level of generalization that the reader must have his doubts. The picture of materialism depends on unsupported statements like the following:

> Metaphysical speculation was never relevant to the harsh physical world of the pioneer colonist, be he farmer, clerk or auctioneer. The man who could concentrate his attention on day-to-day reality was the one who survived in a colonial society where the struggle for uplift was severe and the emotional and material penalties for failure great.[10]

This is mere assertion until the author demonstrates what individual farmers, clerks and auctioneers were thinking, and until he puts his social analysis on a deeper level than his examination of Toowoomba's churches and schools: 'Eight churches and the Downs' first and last synagogue provided consolation, salvation and social satisfaction, nine schools provided varying quantities and qualities of education . . . '[11]

The ideals of the 'town bourgeoisie', we are told, were 'urban-English derived from the England of the great Victorian industrial cities of the Midlands, South East Lancashire and the West Riding of Yorkshire'.[12] But why? and how? What were those English ideals? And how coherent were they if derived from cities so disparate? More important, what were the ideals of the various townsmen of the Downs? It is surely necessary to demonstrate clearly how the relationship with even a generalized industrial England could be very close in a population so mixed and in an economy and polity so different. These Australian towns were transport centres and markets. Their preoccupa-

---

seems to be that they were one and the same. But when talking about politics (p. 285) he seems to take country-town radicalism more seriously.

9 Ibid., pp. 68-70.

10 Ibid., p. 67.

11 Ibid., p. 82. It is useful to set this against an account of the educational assumptions of the time in England. See J. F. C. Harrison, *Learning and Living*, London 1961, Chapter V.

12 Ibid., p. 67.

tions and their class structures were unlike anything in England. Their wealthier inhabitants, according to Waterson, though without any reference to census data, were Protestants from England, Ireland and Scotland, with a sizeable Jewish minority and a small Roman Catholic element.[13] The point is an important one. Towns grow, and in growing develop their own ethos. Strands of it are no doubt derivative, but it varies according to the social, religious, and national composition of the inhabitants. Other strands—and the difficulty again is to detect them—are no doubt indigenous, such as aspects of the bushman's ethos described by Russel Ward.

Towns are also complex organisms. It is not possible to make sense of them without studying them in a conceptually demanding way, with reference to their economies, their demography, their social organization and the behaviour of a fair cross-section of their citizens. No easy matter, that, especially within the compass of a regional history, but let us at least avoid stereotypes. A more inductive study of society might alter Dr Waterson's interpretation of politics on the Downs. As it stands at present, a sober, earnest bourgeois society returned a radical like W. H. Groom to Parliament, and continued to return him.[14] This suggests that the author's definition of 'radical' needs clarifying or his characterization of the town is faulty—or both.[15] He does not ask what Toowoomba had to be radical about, though regional interests seem a possibility, nor does he invoke his view of this town deriving its inspiration from the industrial cities of England where wealth and reform often went hand in hand, and where sober, industrious, self-improving, religious radicalism was rife. What one really needs to know is just what Toowoomba's society was like, in detail and in all its aspects. An impressionistic treatment leaves the reader fumbling for his connections, however sure of his own the author may be.

Similarly, the influence of town hinterlands on political and social attitudes is suggested rather than studied. Dr Waterson does not clearly distinguish between the relationship of Toowoomba to its hinterland, where farming was a success, and the situation at Dalby where it was a failure. He is unsympathetic to storekeepers, whose grub-staking advances to selectors were about as fruitful as the few stalks of wheat on the selectors' land. Considering the risks they ran, which sound more appropriate to kind-hearted fools than hard-headed Shylocks, a purely

[13] Ibid., p. 69.

[14] Ibid., pp. 225-33.

[15] One of the disconcerting things about this book is that the characterization changes. On pages 264-5 a picture of concensus is given which seems remote from earlier accounts of town society, and which makes the radicalism more credible.

economic study would probably reveal that on loans to selectors on marginal land their charges were too low.[16] Their insolvency rate would be a good guide to their bona fides and an indication of the nature of the relationship of country towns with the regional economy. These criticisms should not be allowed to distract attention from the impressive overall plan of the book. The chapter on the towns serves as a reference point for the development of other urban chapters on 'Storekeepers and Banks', 'Millers', and 'Politicians'. It is in fact the most imaginative attempt so far to fit towns into Australian history.

Comprehensive surveys of regional towns can be found in G. L. Buxton, *The Riverina, 1861-1891* (Melbourne 1967) and R. B. Walker, *Old New England* (Sydney 1966). They lack Waterson's fervour and sociological interests, but in offering a less interpretative approach they provide more basic material. Buxton, for instance, in tables and text, shows how the populations of Riverina towns varied according to religion, birthplace and sex, and he identifies their individuality at a close level of public and private behaviour through descriptions like those of James Taylor's life at Deniliquin and the Narrandera Chinese camp. Both authors offer important explanations of the initial growth of towns in a pastoral society. A fascinating aspect of this is the way in which the need for justice not only helped to establish towns as a focus of settlement but also provided ground for conflict between squatters and townsmen. Until 1858 at Armidale nine out of ten magistrates were squatters or overseers for squatters. Then, with the arrival of a police magistrate, the pro-squatter Clerk of Petty Sessions was dismissed and two townsmen were put on the Bench.

This event confirms a trend of town development which G. C. Evans notices at Colac, from squatter dominance to parity and finally to townsman dominance of almost all institutions. The pace of change was often determined by the development of agriculture in the hinterland. Buxton sees the towns initially as rallying places for the rural community, but they soon developed a life of their own (which, incidentally, would have extended their possibilities as rallying places). In both these histories more could be made of the relationship between town and country, possibly by discussing more systematically the variations between towns and the processes by which town and country were linked. The information is often provided; it is just discussion of it that is lacking. Dr Buxton does, however, provide many insights. He sees, and to a great extent explains, the tendency of Deniliquin to go protectionist and to favour federation; of Balranald to remain a squatter town; of

[16] G. Blainey, *Gold and Paper*, Melbourne 1958, p. 95, points out that the National Bank found 10 per cent interest barely remunerative on the best wheat land in Victoria. And that relates to carefully selected clients.

Albury, where small farmers were thick, to be antipathetic to Labour; and of Wagga Wagga, the most heterogeneous of these electorates, to be politically complex. At Wagga Wagga, the shearing gangs congregated before setting out for the stations. There the radical *Hummer* was published. But there also were merchants and stock and station agents linked to squatting, and in the 'eighties millers and entrepreneurs who depended on the rapid expansion of grain growing in the district. To do more than this would involve an appreciation of the economy and society of each town, which it could be argued is the work of local not regional history.

Social history is a special concern of both Walker and Buxton. Compare the latter on drinking with Waterson's treatment of it,[17] and notice his account of hospitals, at Deniliquin in particular.[18] Out of these descriptions the different rhythms of pastoral and agricultural towns emerge. Even so Walker and Buxton are often perfunctory, like amiable gazeteers. Baptists are said to be 'active' in a town, squatters play polo and circuses arrive. But surely what matters is who were the Baptists or squatters (or any group) and what did they do; when did circuses visit and how were they patronized by townsmen and countrymen? The mere enumeration of activities is a misleading shorthand, although simple information of this kind can be skilfully used to distinguish one town from another or to illuminate the patterns of behaviour of townsmen as a whole, as indeed Walker usually makes his details do.

The problem of giving social significance to otherwise insignificant detail is not resolved by practising on the details. Without a more conceptual approach there is little prospect of improvement in the understanding of regional history and particularly of its urban content. In this connection it is worth considering Eric Lampard's suggestion that we approach urban history from three salients, the demographic, the structural, and the behavioural.

> The first deals with the growth and distribution of the population in space; the second pertains to the organization of communities and society; the third has reference to the conduct of individuals. Although structural and behavioural characteristics provide essential clues to the nature and direction of social change, the demographic approach appears to offer at once the least ambiguity and the most promise from the standpoint of observation and measurement. As Schumpeter remarked 'We need statistics not only for explaining

[17] Waterson, p. 71; Buxton, pp. 80-2, 230-1.
[18] Buxton, pp. 83-6, 231-3.

things, but in order to know precisely what there is to be explained'.[19]

This approach, which is similar to the geographers' concern with locational studies, service categories, central business districts and population densities, can be valuable in helping to construct a typology of towns. Thus, some of the basic characteristics Meinig identified in South Australian wheat towns could be further refined and then compared with wheat, squatting, mining or mixed-economy towns elsewhere in Australia and overseas.

A comparative base is naturally only the beginning of wisdom. Once something like it is achieved, however, the way is open for a new series of questions. How significant is the low proportion of Wesleyans in Riverina towns, compared with the gold towns of the Western District and the wheat towns of South Australia? How does one interpret a high percentage of Roman Catholics or a predominantly male population? How 'alien' are the different types of towns from their hinterlands in terms of religion, birthplace, age structure and education? To what extent are town characteristics a function of size, age or location? How are political divisions related to the social and economic structures of towns?

Whatever the outcome of such questions they cannot be answered until our towns have been described more carefully. Statistics alone are not enough. A useful model is Richard Wade's treatment of the cities of the American middle-west in *The Urban Frontier* (Harvard 1959), which avoids interpretive fireworks but provides a framework for them. Wade explores systematically the multiple characteristics of his cities and puts them into the wider contexts of the rural frontier, the eastern seaboard and the Mississippi River.

For our purposes the classic American methodological example may still be Merle Curti's *The Making of an American Community* (California 1959). Curti builds up from individual census files a comprehensive picture of a slice of the American frontier. We have no comparable source but despite excellent ratebook collections in many towns, we tend to follow a less analytical, more genteel English tradition exemplified by Asa Briggs. Historians are often unaware of the nature of the information contained in ratebooks, which do, however, vary considerably from place to place. Topics which can be investigated with their help include home ownership, occupations, social mobility, building materials, industrial, commercial and residential location, land use and land speculation. The fortunes of migrant groups can be

[19] Lampard, E., 'Urbanization and Social Change: on Broadening the Scope and Relevance of Urban History' in O. Handlin and J. Burchard, *The Historian and the City*, Massachusetts 1966, p. 238.

traced by surname; in fact ratebooks are probably one of the most valuable untapped sources for advancing the study of the Chinese in Australia. Because they are revised annually they give a closer-textured view of social change than the census does, and it is this quality which led Graeme Davison to use them as the base for an important chapter of his recent ANU PhD thesis, *The Rise and Fall of 'Marvellous Melbourne', 1880-1895*, a work which is sure to become the inspiration of further studies of urban life in Australia. His treatment of urban experience will undoubtedly influence historians of country towns, who may of course weep for their comparative lack of letters, personal papers, printed reminiscences, business records and short biographies.

People are the main victims of this weakness of local source material. Lampard's behavioural salient is easier to achieve at a fairly general level such as Margaret Kiddle's Western District. She was able to bring the squatters to life because there were many to choose from and because of the stability of pastoral families. For Walker, Buxton, Waterson, Priestley and others, when dealing with towns, especially small towns, the task is not easy. Some historians, like Margaret Kiddle, have an eye for the apt character study and can use the experiences of individuals to strengthen their generalizations. This is true of Susan Priestley and G. L. Buxton. Echuca's Hopwood and Deniliquin's Taylor are rounded characters as well as symbols or symptoms of their place and time. Other writers, and Duncan Waterson has been gently chided for it, depict types not people.[20] Others again, present a scissors-and-paste parade of individuals without trying to establish how representative they were.

One of the toughest general problems is putting people and places into context. Historians should get the cultural context straight, as Professor La Nauze has warned us.[21] Whether that means seeing our history as part of British history, or world economic development, the principle is the same. We need also to be aware of inter-regional and intra-regional contrasts and comparisons. And this is where the development of a typology of towns and the more systematic treatment of regions can help us to achieve wider perspectives.

Of course it is not just the system that counts. Insight can be equally valuable. There is a passage in Buxton's book which suddenly illuminates a facet of frontier life, and it comes from an awareness of context.[22] It concerns the difference between the Victorian and New South Wales police forces, the former centralized and efficient, the latter localized and a shambles. And this was an important condition

[20] *Historical Studies*, No. 52, p. 577, a review by W. K. Hancock.
[21] 'The Study of Australian History 1929-1959', *Historical Studies*, No. 33.
[22] Op. cit., p. 76.

under which towns developed. More strongly, our awareness of context greatly affects the framing of our hypotheses. It may not be possible to write a good history of Sydney without knowing the history of Melbourne. After all a point alters in context. Notice what happens to a simple statement,

Event X occurred at Sydney in 1858, therefore . . .

if one notices also that

X did not occur at Melbourne until 1875

or

X never occurred at Melbourne

or

X did not occur anywhere else in the world.

An event takes explanatory force from its context. To know whether it was usual or unusual is to be a step along the road towards the framing of a useful hypothesis.[23]

Greater concern for context may lead us to modify some of our conclusions. The 'dog-eat-dog' situation of town and country in specific regions at specific times may be an index of inter-regional pressures like those that Dr Waterson describes on the Darling Downs. Cheaper South Australian and Victorian grain subjected the region to divisive pressures, which may not be accurately labelled in terms of the region itself. The farmers failure to compete forced the storekeepers to raise their commissions and interest charges. Thus a general approach suggests a particular hypothesis which, when tested, throws light back on the generalization. It would be interesting to know whether (and why) the New England townsman won or lost in backing the selector, and whether the divisive tendency noticed by Waterson also existed in Walker's territory.

Whatever the answer, it has to be fitted into a general picture of capital formation in agriculture, much of which, according to traditional accounts, seems to have been channelled through small townsmen—except in South Australia where banks and large commercial interests were important, and in Victoria where the National Bank strongly supported selection in the 1870s.[24] Unfortunately, however, the general picture is not available. Although the agricultural component according to Butlin was not far behind the pastoral component in the growth of gross domestic product,[25] his monumental work contains few references to it and no special study of agricultural capital formation

[23] See H. Stretton, *The Political Sciences*, London 1969, pp. 245-52.

[24] G. Blainey, op. cit., pp. 94-5.

[25] N. G. Butlin, *Investment in Australian Economic Development 1861-1900*, Cambridge 1964, p. 16.

like that provided for the pastoral industry. Local and regional historians will probably have to provide the evidence before anything can be done to assess this aspect of capital formation at all accurately.

Economic historians of Australia pre-Butlin provided the flimsiest of frameworks for the study of towns. And Butlin's contribution is only a first step, limited as it is for more general purposes by its emphasis on growth and by the use of population figures as an index of urban growth. He notices, for instance, that of 34 Victorian towns that were reasonably important in urban growth only three grew throughout the three decades, 1861-91. Eleven were spent by 1871 and many 'retired into a semi-rural slumber from which they failed to awaken during the nineteenth century'.[26] Professor Butlin sees the growth of the gold towns in the 'sixties as the result of the after effects of gold mining and the commercial-industrial utilization of an erstwhile goldmining population. But this is misleading for quite a number of them. Gold mining was strong in the 'sixties and perhaps more heavily capitalized than it had ever been. And in Ballarat when it fell away in the 'seventies within the city boundaries, discoveries in the hinterland encouraged an outward movement of miners, who were replaced, often in new housing locations, by skilled newcomers. At this time the metal industry was developing rapidly, the central business area was being reconstructed and the housing stock added to dramatically.

Mere population numbers are no measure of that kind of urban growth. They can also be very misleading in comparing the towns of different regions. The age-sex structure of pastoral, agricultural and mining towns may differ significantly and thus affect their economic potential. Work force studies can be important, especially where jobs exist for women. Intercensal changes of occupational groupings can alter calculations of income. The wealth flowing into a town from its hinterland may vastly increase the town's income and spending without affecting its size. Ballarat is a case in point. The bonanza of deep alluvial mining in the years 1865-8 confirmed Ballarat as an investment centre. It already had a strong legal community whose members had been closely connected with mining and who were prominent not only in the stock market but in channelling mortgage investment. In the 'seventies and 'eighties their control of funds helped to support the Wimmera and Mallee wheat farmers. Their own fortunes stimulated a completely new class of building in Ballarat.

Whether or not this kind of growth was paralleled in Wagga Wagga, Albury, Armidale, Toowoomba, Townsville and Charters Towers is certainly worth discussing. It seems unlikely that it was matched by

[26] Ibid., pp. 186-7.

any of the minor towns of New South Wales and Queensland, which Butlin catches in his net by defining 'urban' as 500+ people, and which typically grew by say 100 between censuses and added to the building stock twenty-five shanties of split palings, a few stores, a bank, a butcher's shop and a handful of brick and weatherboard houses.[27] Another aspect of the difference between the towns of Victoria and New South Wales is the way the Victorian gold towns initiated development in their hinterlands, whereas towns in New South Wales tended to respond to hinterland development achieved from outside the region, as, for instance, through the migration of selectors from Victoria and South Australia.

The chief obstacle to the development of regional urban studies is just this difficulty of studying town economies. Dr Buxton makes an attempt at a general economic framework for his towns, but none of the other books mentioned in this review has even identified the problem. Waterson's failure to do so cuts away the ground from under his social analysis and Walker's virtual omission of the economy gives parts of his study of the towns a scissors-and-paste quality.

It seems to me that local, regional and general urban history should be advancing along the same broad front. I would modify the salients suggested by Lampard to include economics, and would like to see far more research into the techniques and concepts appropriate to the various aspects of Australian history. At the same time it is natural that within any suggested framework individual historians should develop a variety of emphases, according to their interests and subjects. In suggesting that the time has come for a greater maturity of concepts, I am aware that this is related to the formal development of research. Regional studies are only in their infancy. What their authors lack in skill and understanding is mainly a reflection of the primitive state of the historical industry. But now that there is a number of models, I think individual historians should be aiming at a clarity of purpose akin to Meinig's, Curti's and Wade's. Historians should try to make explicit just what they are or are not doing. They should be aware of their place in the advancing frontier. Above all, perhaps, they should at present carry a torch for local history as the general history of a locality, needing its own monographs, defining its own structures—despite the fact that the evidence is rarely deposited in favour of local generalization.

There is a final related problem. We have to remember that urban history is close-grained. Its study is by nature multi-disciplinary, for the techniques of geography, demography, sociology and economics—to

[27] This is hypothetical and biased. But the point is that it could be true.

name but a few—are needed if cities and towns are to be effectively analysed and described. This being so, urban historians should work, ideally, with other specialists before beginning their brand of generalizing. And if such co-operation is not possible, I can see only two alternatives. Historians either try to sketch in some of that other work for themselves or treat events as if they are flat rather than rounded, which is putting the clock back rather a long way.[28]

It might be wise at this point to psychoanalyse the author of this review. What he has said about other people's work is gratuitous and unkind. What he wants is surely impossible. What he would suggest as a minimum approach is clearly unpleasant, if not confusing. Yet what road is there for an urban historian to follow? The towns are there in all their complexity. What point is there in simplifying them into something else?

[28] See Stretton, op. cit., Chapter 3.

Sean Glynn

APPROACHES TO URBAN HISTORY: THE CASE FOR CAUTION*

The function of social science is quite different from that of the natural sciences—it is to provide society with an organ of self-consciousness.[1]

Joan Robinson

I

It has been truly said 'to assert the importance of urbanization is a beginning, not an end'.[2] In recent years historians of all kinds in many countries have been led by social scientists into a rapidly growing interest in urban history, and this volume is a record of the first full conference of urban historians held in Britain. This is an appropriate time and place to examine the findings of the conference and to discuss the lessons, both positive and negative, that may be drawn by Australian urban historians.

Of the 43 participants at the conference, historians and economic historians heavily outnumbered geographers, sociologists, and others—including a solitary Professor of English. The printed record includes 16 papers and reports based on tape-recordings of seven discussion sessions. The two main areas of concern were the materials and methods of urban historical study, and the comparative study of British cities. Despite the wide range of views represented, it is noteworthy that, apart from a few concluding comments by Professor S. G. Checkland, the economic approach is conspicuously absent. At its most constructive, the debate is one between sociologists and conventional historians. It might also be said that at least half of the papers are concerned with issues which constitute, or relate to, urban history only in the incidental sense. The net of urban history has been stretched to contain

* A review of H. J. Dyos (ed.), *The Study of Urban History: The proceedings of an International Round-Table Conference of the Urban History Group at Gilbert Murray Hall, University of Leicester on 23-26 September, 1966*, Edward Arnold, London 1968, pp. xxii + 400: 90*s* stg.

1 *Freedom and Necessity*, London 1970, p. 120.

2 P. Laslett in E. A. Wrigley (ed.), *Introduction to English Historical Demography*, London 1966.

traditional and novel studies carried out by people who would probably not regard themselves primarily as urban historians.

In his foreword to the book Asa Briggs writes that 'there is not one valid approach to urban history but many' (p. 14). This point is taken up by Dyos in his 'Agenda for Urban Historians', when he poses, but manifestly fails to answer, the question: 'Is this the stage in the development of *the subject* when we should be concentrating our efforts on carefully chosen lines of research, or should we simply encourage every original idea and applaud every virtuoso performance? (p. 3, my italics). It seems that Dyos, not without some methodological regrets and pangs of conscience, has decided on the latter course. At present, at least, it would appear that urban history cannot be a clearly definable entity with its own distinctive approach. The only viable approach must be a broad multi-disciplinary and inter-disciplinary one—with all the attendant problems and pitfalls—extending beyond the social sciences. Thus we are subjected to an eloquent if tenuous case for an academic 'come-all-ye' of urban history of the kind seen in successive issues of the British *Urban History Newsletter*.[3] The question which remains, particularly for Australian study, is whether or not the Dyos type of approach is the only alternative to the horror of yet another arbitrarily demarcated and jargonized 'discipline' embracing a rigorously defined version of urban history? This consideration will be taken up later.

Dyos follows his general comments with a useful historiographical and bibliographical survey[4] and ends on the correct note by stating with typical candour and accuracy that 'the field is as yet a very ragged one and those in it are not a little confused as to what they are doing' (p. 46). The next paper, by Francois Bedarida, surveys French urban historiography and research, and presents some sceptical views about urban studies in general and the viability of an inter-disciplinary approach. On a more mundane level, Dyos (with A. B. M. Baker) and W. A. Armstrong present papers dealing with the application of the computer to census data. Armstrong is concerned primarily with the use of census enumerator's books and Dyos with more general applications. The former should be particularly useful to historians who have not fully appreciated the enormous possibilities of historical data handling by computer. Clearly the computer is destined to be a vital tool in this field, but one is left with the fear that the availability of 'computer-prone' data may dominate the approach which, in turn, may

[3] Edited by H. J. Dyos from the University of Leicester and issued twice yearly.

[4] Part of which has already appeared in his 'The Growth of Cities in the Nineteenth Century: A Review of Recent Writing', *Victorian Studies*, Vol. IX, No. 3 (March 1966), pp. 225-37.

not pose and attempt to answer the most interesting questions about the urbanization process.[5]

The case for using town plans in the study of urban history is overstated by M. R. G. Conzen with a confidence which is perhaps more characteristic of geographers than of historians and social scientists, and F. H. W. Sheppard describes the frankly antiquarian and architecturally-orientated 'Survey of London' which has been in progress, however unspectacularly, since the late nineteenth century.[6] Contributions by G. H. Martin[7] and F. M. Jones[8] present a visual approach to towns and cities, making excellent use of 54 illustrations and indicating that the camera, in skilled hands, may rival the computer as a tool of urban history. Martin, who ostensibly attempts to discover historical influence in the outward and visible appearance of towns, rather than in their archives, will probably be less relevant to Australian historians than Jones, who aims 'to describe some of the characteristics of an environment and the manner in which it would have been possible for human beings to adapt to it and create compensatory situations, or find escapes, however temporary' (p. 171). His impressionistic but ingenious attempts to explain how the urban Victorians were able to escape and compensate for noise, dirt and smells in their environment, make that era seem much brighter and less aesthetically barren than it appears in the popular imagination. Whether or not Jones, as an architect, sees things which do not meet, and would not have met, the ordinary eye is debatable but his contribution is an important reminder that urban history should not be solely the preserve of social scientists. This type of approach in Australian urban history could yield fascinating results.

Leo F. Schnore's paper[9] may leave the suspicion that urban sociology, which dates back to the 'Chicago School' of the 1890s is, to use one of his own phrases, 'a kind of common-sense rationalisation' at best and, in its less fortunate manifestations, a barren approach with pretentious overtones. Schnore classifies urban sociology into behavioural, structural, ecological and demographic divisions and suggests that the latter two, being the easiest to approach, are the most fruitful for the historian.

[5] According to Armstrong, who is clearly an historical demographer rather than an urban historian in the strict sense, 'a growing volume of careful analysis will enable us to measure the intensity of "obvious" relationships as they varied between time and place—and sometimes we may be able to discover new ones' (p. 85).

[6] 'The object now might be defined as to trace the topographical and architectural history of a given area . . . ' (p. 133).

[7] 'The Town as Palimpsest.'

[8] 'The Aesthetic of the Nineteenth-Century Industrial Town.'

[9] Under the rather misleading title 'Problems in the Quantitative Study of Urban History'.

He considers, however, that history *per se* is inadequate and that each social science must develop an historical approach in the light of its own interests and methods.

Marshall's[10] discussion of small industrial settlements in nineteenth-century Lancashire suggests themes which might be pursued in Australian history. In particular, the relationship between stages of urban growth and the fortunes of particular industries–a well-known phenomenon in Australian town evolution–and his suggestion that (in early Victorian Lancashire) 'it is a mistake to assume, whether in terms of urban boundaries or of social life, a sharp town-country antithesis' (pp. 223-4). His paper also presents a reminder that industrialization and urbanization are not necessarily and always intimately associated. Carter[11] presents a seven-stage synopsis of town growth in Wales since Anglo-Norman times and concludes that 'Urbanism is a phenomenon which demands study as a whole. The urban fabric, layout, build and function, is an epitome of the varied forces which have been brought to bear on the town over a long period of growth. This demands, at some stage, a synoptic viewpoint which, if it leads on the one hand to generalisation and superficiality, on the other places in perspective the detailed investigation of more limited aspects' (p. 252).

In a solitary paper on suburban development D. A. Reeder[12] examines the changing populations, occupational structure and social status of a group of suburbs dependent on central London. We do not at this stage know whether analogous patterns may be evident in Australia, but clearly there is a need for studies of this kind. Perhaps the most interesting implication of this paper is that suburban evolution is a rather more complex phenomenon than is often supposed.

Probably the most stimulating paper is John Foster's[13] attempt at an empirical testing of Marxist theory by comparing the degree of class-consciousness in three medium-sized nineteenth-century towns–Oldham ('at mid-century there were 12,000 worker families selling their labour to 70 capitalist families'), Northampton and South Shields–between which he reveals sharp contrasts. In terms of Foster's approach, class-consciousness is a reflection of urban physical, social and economic conditions including spatial proximity, the structure and composition of capital ownership and the capitalist *élite,* and the socio-economic condition of the wage-earning class. A comparison of levels of class-consciousness is, therefore, a convenient and meaningful way of com-

[10] 'Colonisation as a factor in the Planting of Towns in North-West England.'
[11] 'Phases of Town Growth in Wales.'
[12] 'A Theatre of Suburbs: Some Patterns of Development in West London, 1801-1911.'
[13] 'Nineteenth-Century Towns—A Class Dimension.'

paring towns as a whole. Not surprisingly, this paper provoked much discussion and little agreement.

The account by R. Newton[14] of changes in the governing *élite* of Exeter, a quiet and uninteresting if not a typical Victorian town, seems rather less relevant than E. P. Hennock's[15] examination of city councillors in Leeds and Birmingham during the same period. Hennock's attempt to discover 'to what extent were municipal corporations . . . able to draw on the services of those most prominent in the economic and social life of the town?' (p. 316) is an obvious but important line of inquiry, in no way unique to urban history nor novel to Australian historians. In a final paper, S. G. Checkland attempts to move 'Towards a Definition of Urban History' and a 'methodological summing-up'.

II

This volume is a useful compendium of ideas and a fair sample of work in progress in British urban history. Australian historians who in recent years have commenced their own version of 'rural-urban drift' will share some of the interests and problems of their British counterparts in moving into a complex and unfamiliar area. Nevertheless, one is conscious in reading this volume of important differences between British and Australian urban phenomena, and of the need for Australian urban history to develop, at least to some extent, its own theory and method rather than slavishly following overseas trends. The British process whereby a predominantly agricultural population was drawn into urban centres as a result of population growth, increasing industrialization and changes in the rural sector, was to some extent reversed in Australia in that urbanization developed in advance of rural settlement and was an important influence in promoting it. These and other variations suggest that important questions in Australian urban history may be quite different from those raised in Britain.

In attempting to define urban sociology Schnore referred to a field without focus, which concerned itself with the sociological aspects of anything that happens in cities: the study of social behaviour in an urban locale. At the present time, the only feasible attempts to define urban history must be equally vague and unsatisfactory. Urban history as the study of anything which has happened in or to towns or cities avoids the question of what we mean by the term 'urbanization'; it may indeed be a way of avoiding a direct and meaningful examination of the phenomenon. Urbanization, like the 'Industrial Revolution', is the focus of many problems but, as Briggs has warned, there may be

[14] 'Society and Politics in Exeter, 1837-1914.'
[15] 'The Social Composition of Borough Councils in Two Large Cities 1835-1914.'

a danger in pivoting too much on the city. It might be argued that in order to develop and justify itself fully as a clearly defined and worthwhile field of study, urban history requires what must amount to an 'urban interpretation' of history. This type of approach would have to be grounded in the hypothesis that urbanization was, in part at least, an independent rather than a dependent variable in history. Such a view is indeed possible: economic development, including industrialization, may be seen as a consequence as well as a cause of urbanization, and in the social field the consequences of urbanization seem endless.[16] On the other hand, the conventional view of urbanization as a dependent variable seems well-established amongst economists and economic historians.

One of the most important questions raised in this volume came from a sociologist, R. E. Pah, who asked whether ' . . . the adoption of urban living forms itself constituted urbanisation . . . Is "urbanisation" the way that one suburb or one village coalesces with another? Is it a change in the "way of life"? . . . Does place have a fundamental sociological significance?' (p. 274). Any attempt to answer these questions is likely to lead to the conclusion that the different social sciences are likely to adopt different definitions of urbanization, and so describe the city as the blind men described the elephant. From the point of view of the economist and economic historian the methodological problem is, possibly, less complex. Most economists since Adam Smith have appreciated the relationship between urbanization and economic development. Marx, for example, declared that 'the foundation of every division of labour that is well developed and brought about by the exchange of commodities is the separation between town and country'.[17] Urbanization is possible only in an economy which has produced an agricultural 'surplus' and progressed beyond the subsistence level towards a high degree of occupational specialization and exchange. The development of non-agricultural economic pursuits, which tend to use relatively small areas of land simply as sites rather than as inputs to the productive process, leads to a more mobile economy in the locational sense. Since most secondary and tertiary activities can facilitate specialization and derive economies by operating in close spatial proximity to other processes, transport facilities, markets and input sources including labour, there is inevitably a close connection between economic development and urbanization. If urbanization is simply the spatial human and physical pattern resulting from (and dependent on) economic development, then economists

[16] A recent example of this kind of approach may be seen in Jane Jacobs, *The Economy of Cities*, London 1970.

[17] *Capital* (Humbolt ed.), p. 212.

and economic historians should continue to focus primarily on their traditional interest in economic growth and leave 'urbanization' to other disciplines.

Unfortunately, such a simple solution, particularly for Australian historians, is unlikely to arise. In Australia it is possible to argue that the city created the agricultural 'surplus' by promoting rural settlement and specialization in rural production *ab initio*; and even in areas where the pattern of development took a more conventional form, the traditional view of urbanization as a dependent economic variable is under attack. There is at present a growing awareness on the part of many Australian historians of a need to rewrite national and local history in ways which take account of urbanization.[18] There is also a growing dissatisfaction in relation to the narrow, rigid and esoteric version of economic history which has been evident in recent years and the relatively trivial and non-empirical nature of much social and general history. The main hope lies in a breed which Dyos has described as 'younger historians more inclined to get hold of problems just as they are, pursuing them with whatever means seem best, however unfamiliar at first sight, and in whatever company they find themselves'. The need, in other words, is for a flexible, eclectic and empirical approach.

If the keynote of future historical research is to be synthesis and interdisciplinary study, then urbanization will be a natural venue for different kinds of scholars including historians. Checkland has pointed out that there have been three principal forms of study undertaken by British urban historians—secular trends, thematic aspects, and contextual studies. It seems reasonable to expect a similar pattern in Australia. Checkland uses the British *Urban History Newsletter* to indicate the wide range of thematic aspects already under investigation: housing, buildings, land use, land tenure, transportation, administration, finance, politics, health, sanitation, food supplies, population, family, social class, *élites*, power-structure, subcultures, crime, conflict, protest, philanthropy, welfare, architecture, spatial planning, the demands of terrain, the aesthetics of the city, locational advantage, the industrial mix, and the commercial facilities of the central business district (pp. 351-2). Many of these aspects have already been investigated in the Australian context, often by people who would hardly regard themselves as urban historians. In a country which was (statistically) defined as being two-thirds urban by 1890, it is very difficult indeed to undertake any broad piece of historical research which does not throw some light on what Dyos refers to as 'the subject' of urban history.

[18] This need has already been emphasized by N. G. Butlin in *Investment in Australian Economic Development, 1861-1900*, Cambridge 1964. See also Sean Glynn, *Urbanisation in Australian History*, Melbourne 1970.

Nevertheless, it might still be argued that there is an urgent need for a frontal assault on urbanization in Australian history: giving attention to what Checkland has categorized as contextual and secular studies. While the basic premise for such an argument—the all-pervading importance of urbanization—may be acceptable, the feasibility of this approach remains in question. Australian economic and social historians are relatively few and many fundamental questions remain unanswered in their traditional areas of interest, which must surely be considered before any substantial diversion of interests and resources is contemplated. The entire field of Australian demographic history has remained almost untouched since Coghlan; we know little about the history of manufacturing or building, particularly in the nineteenth century; some of the most important problems in Australian history are social rather than economic, yet there is scarcely an example of an attempt to examine the historical aspects of Australian society and social structure in the light of modern sociological methods. Any attempt to understand the general phenomenon of urbanization in Australian history, without prior investigation and understanding of these and other questions, must run the risk of being a relatively wasteful diversion of effort. Dyos has said that 'urban history is the most newly discovered continent and into the scramble for it goes every kind of explorer' (p. 6). This current issue of *AEHR* notwithstanding, Australian historians must make sure that they have encompassed the Cumberland Plains before they embark on a collective trip to what might become their Cooper's Creek.